To

_____

From

_____

Date

_____

# 365-DAY JOURNAL
# FOOD, FITNESS, AND FAITH
## FOR WOMEN

*The quoted ideas expressed in this book (but not Scripture verses) are not, in all cases, exact quotations, as some have been edited for clarity and brevity. In all cases, the author has attempted to maintain the speaker's original intent. In some cases, quoted material for this book was obtained from secondary sources, primarily print media. While every effort was made to ensure the accuracy of these sources, the accuracy cannot be guaranteed. For additions, deletions, corrections, or clarifications in future editions of this text, please write Freeman-Smith, LLC.*

Scripture quotations are taken from:

. The Holy Bible, King James Version (KJV)

The Holy Bible, New International Version (NIV) Copyright © 1973, 1978, 1984, by International Bible Society. Used by permission of Zondervan Publishing House. All rights reserved.

The Holy Bible, New King James Version (NKJV) Copyright © 1982 by Thomas Nelson, Inc. Used by permission.

Holy Bible, New Living Translation, (NLT) copyright © 1996. Used by permission of Tyndale House Publishers, Inc., Wheaton, Illinois 60189. All rights reserved.

The Message (MSG)- This edition issued by contractual arrangement with NavPress, a division of The Navigators, U.S.A. Originally published by NavPress in English as THE MESSAGE: The Bible in Contemporary Language copyright 2002-2003 by Eugene Peterson. All rights reserved.

New Century Version®. (NCV) Copyright © 1987, 1988, 1991 by Word Publishing, a division of Thomas Nelson, Inc. All rights reserved. Used by permission.

The New American Standard Bible®, (NASB) Copyright © 1960, 1962, 1963, 1968, 1971, 1972, 1973, 1975, 1977, 1995 by The Lockman Foundation. Used by permission.

The Holman Christian Standard Bible™ (HCSB) Copyright © 1999, 2000, 2001 by Holman Bible Publishers. Used by permission.

Cover Design by Kim Russell / Wahoo Designs
Page Layout by Bart Dawson

ISBN 978-1-60587-307-7

# 365-DAY JOURNAL
# FOOD,
# FITNESS,
# AND FAITH
## FOR WOMEN

# A MESSAGE TO READERS

*A wise man will hear and increase learning, and a man of understanding will attain wise counsel.*

The advice in this book is general in nature, and your circumstances are specific to you. For that reason, we strongly suggest that you consult your physician before beginning any new regimen of physical exercise or diet. Don't depend upon this book—or any other book like it—to be your sole source of information on matters pertaining to your health. Instead, consider Proverbs 1:5 and seek wise counsel from a variety of sources, especially your personal physician, before making major health-related decisions.

# INTRODUCTION

God has a plan for every aspect of your life, including your food, your fitness, and your faith. But God will not force His plans upon you; to the contrary, He has given you the ability to make choices. The consequences of those choices help determine the quality and the tone of your life. This journaling book is intended to help you make wise choices—choices that will lead to spiritual, physical, and emotional health—by encouraging you to rely heavily upon the promises of God's Holy Word.

If you're like most people, you've already tried, perhaps on many occasions, to form healthier habits. You've employed your own willpower in a noble effort to create a new, improved, healthier you. You've probably tried to improve various aspects of your spiritual, physical, or emotional health. Perhaps you've gone on diets, or made New Year's resolutions, or tried the latest self-help fad in an attempt to finally make important changes in your life. And if you're like most folks, you've been successful . . . for a while. But eventually, those old familiar habits came creeping back into your life, and the improvements that you had made proved to be temporary. This book is intended to help you build a series of healthy habits for your Christian walk . . . and make those habits stick.

During the next 365 days, you will be asked to depend less upon your own willpower and more upon God's power as you establish healthier habits. As you take steps to enhance your spiritual, emotional, and physical health, these pages will help, but they offer no shortcuts. Healthy living is a journey, not a destination, and that journey requires discipline. If you're willing to make the step-by-step journey toward improved health, rest assured that God is taking careful note of your progress . . . and He's quietly urging you to take the next step.

# DAY 1

## 365 DAYS TO A NEW AND IMPROVED YOU

*A prudent person foresees the danger ahead and takes precautions. The simpleton goes blindly on and suffers the consequences.*

Proverbs 27:12 NLT

You are embarking on a grand adventure. This book provides you with the opportunity to record 365 journal entries, one for each day of the year. During the next 12 months, take time each morning to write down your own thoughts about food, faith, and fitness. As you write down your thoughts and formalize your plans, you'll motivate yourself to take the necessary steps to improve your health, your faith, and your life.

In the space below, jot down a few of your most important goals for the year ahead. Remember, if you need more space to write, there are extra pages for that in the back of this book.

_____

_____

_____

_____

_____

_____

# DAY 2

## GOD'S PLAN FOR A HEALTHIER YOU

*You will show me the path of life; in Your presence is fullness of joy; at Your right hand are pleasures forevermore.*

Psalm 16:11 NKJV

Physical fitness, like every other aspect of your life, begins and ends with God. If you'd like to adopt a healthier lifestyle, God is willing to help. In fact, if you sincerely wish to create a healthier you—either physically, emotionally, or spiritually—God is anxious to be your silent partner in that endeavor, but it's up to you to ask for His help.

In the space below, ask God for strength and the courage to follow His plan for your life.

_____

_____

_____

_____

_____

_____

_____

_____

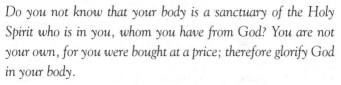

# YOUR BODY:
# A PRICELESS GIFT FROM GOD

*Do you not know that your body is a sanctuary of the Holy Spirit who is in you, whom you have from God? You are not your own, for you were bought at a price; therefore glorify God in your body.*

1 Corinthians 6:19-20 HCSB

If you trust God, and if you keep asking for His help, He can transform your health and your life. If you sincerely ask Him to help you, the same God who created the universe will help you defeat the harmful habits that have heretofore defeated you. So, if at first you don't succeed, keep praying. God is listening, and He's ready to help you become a better person if you ask Him . . . so ask today.

In the space below, thank God for the body He has given you.

_____

_____

_____

_____

_____

_____

_____

## PUTTING GOD FIRST

*But seek first the kingdom of God and His righteousness, and all these things will be provided for you.*

Matthew 6:33 HCSB

One of the quickest ways to accomplish any worthy goal—perhaps the only way—is to do it with God as your partner. So here's a question worth thinking about: Have you made God your top priority by offering Him your heart, your soul, your talents, and your time? Or are you in the habit of giving God little more than a few hours on Sunday morning? The answer to these questions will determine, to a surprising extent, the direction of your day, the quality of your life, and the state of your health.

Think of at least three things you can do today to put God where He belongs: in first place.

_____

_____

_____

_____

_____

_____

_____

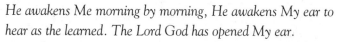

# HAVE A REGULAR
# APPOINTMENT WITH GOD

*He awakens Me morning by morning, He awakens My ear to hear as the learned. The Lord God has opened My ear.*

Isaiah 50:4-5 NKJV

---

Would you like a foolproof formula for a stronger faith and a better life? Here it is: stay in close contact with God. Hannah Whitall Smith wrote, "The crucial question for each of us is this: What do you think of Jesus, and do you yet have a personal acquaintance with Him?" Today, think about your relationship with Jesus: what it is and what it could be.

---

In the space below, write down a few thoughts about the role that Jesus plays in your life.

_____

_____

_____

_____

_____

_____

_____

_____

## RESPECTING YOUR BODY

*Therefore, brothers, by the mercies of God, I urge you to present your bodies as a living sacrifice, holy and pleasing to God; this is your spiritual worship.*

Romans 12:1 HCSB

In the 12th chapter of Romans, Paul encourages us to take special care of the bodies God has given us. But it's tempting to do otherwise. We live in a fast-food world where unhealthy choices are convenient, inexpensive, and tempting. As a result, too many of us find ourselves glued to the television, with a snack in one hand and a clicker in the other. God's Word teaches us to treat our bodies with respect and honor.

Take a few minutes to think about your eating habits. Then, in the space below, grade yourself on the quality and quantity of the foods you usually eat.

_____

_____

_____

_____

_____

_____

_____

# FORMING HEALTHY HABITS

*Dear friend, I pray that you may prosper in every way and be in good health, just as your soul prospers.*

3 John 1:2 HCSB

It's an old saying and a true one: First, you make your habits, and then your habits make you. Some habits will inevitably bring you closer to God; other habits will lead you away from the path He has chosen for you. If you sincerely desire to improve your spiritual health, you must honestly examine the habits that make up the fabric of your day. And you must abandon those habits that are displeasing to God.

Today, ask God to help you form healthier habits. If you ask for His help—if you petition Him sincerely and often—your Heavenly Father will guide your steps and protect you from harmful behaviors.

## YOUR PARTNERSHIP
## WITH GOD

*So now we can rejoice in our wonderful new relationship with God—all because of what our Lord Jesus Christ has done for us in making us friends of God.*

Romans 5:11 NLT

Perhaps you have tended to divide the concerns of your life into two categories: "spiritual" and "other." If so, it's time to reconsider. God intends for you to integrate His commandments into every aspect of your life, and that includes your physical and emotional health, too. Your journey toward improved health can be, and should be, a journey that you make with God.

In the space below, make a pledge to yourself that you'll make God a full partner in your journey to improved health.

_____

_____

_____

_____

_____

_____

_____

# DAY 9

## BETTER FOODS LEAD TO BETTER HEALTH

*Do not remember the former things, nor consider the things of old. Behold, I will do a new thing.*

Isaiah 43:18-19 NKJV

Take a few minutes to examine your eating habits. Do you gobble down snack foods while watching television? If so, stop. Do you drink high-calorie soft drinks or feast on unhealthy snacks like potato chips or candy? If so, you're doing yourself a disservice. Do you load up your plate and then feel obligated to eat every last bite? If so, it's time to form some new habits.

Poor eating habits are usually well established, so they won't be easy to change, but change them you must if you want to enjoy the benefits of a healthy lifestyle.

Today, write down at least three unhealthy foods that you'll eliminate from your diet.

_____

_____

_____

_____

_____

_____

## YOUR CHOICES MATTER

*I am offering you life or death, blessings or curses. Now, choose life! . . . To choose life is to love the Lord your God, obey him, and stay close to him.*

Deuteronomy 30:19-20 NCV

Each day, we make thousands of small choices concerning the things that we do and the things we think. Often, our actions are simply the result of impulse or habit. Do you sincerely seek to improve the overall quality of your health? Then vow to yourself and to God that you will begin making the kind of wise choices that will lead to a longer, healthier, happier life.

In the space below, write down at least five healthy meals that can be prepared at home.

_____

_____

_____

_____

_____

_____

_____

_____

# DAY 11

## HAVE THE COURAGE
## TO TRUST GOD

*Trust in the Lord with all your heart, and do not rely on your own understanding; think about Him in all your ways, and He will guide you on the right paths.*

Proverbs 3:5-6 HCSB

Are you a person who seeks God's blessings for yourself and your family? Then trust Him. Trust Him with your health. Trust Him with your relationships. Trust Him with your priorities. Follow His commandments and pray for His guidance. Trust your Heavenly Father day by day, moment by moment—in good times and in trying times. Then, wait patiently for God's revelations . . . and prepare yourself for the abundance and peace that will most certainly be yours when you do.

Today, jot down at least one important idea about God's plans for your spiritual or physical health.

_____

_____

_____

_____

_____

_____

# DON'T GO ON A DIET,
# CHANGE YOUR LIFESTYLE

*Their end is destruction; their god is their stomach; their glory is in their shame. They are focused on earthly things.*

Philippians 3:19 HCSB

---

If you want to lose weight, don't dare go on a diet! It's a sad fact, but true: in the vast majority of cases, diets simply don't work. In fact, one study that examined the results of popular diets conducted that nearly 100% of dieters suffered almost "complete relapse after 3 to 5 years." In other words, dieters almost always return to their pre-diet weights (or to even higher weight levels). If diets don't work, what should you do if you weigh more than you should? The answer is straightforward: If you need to lose weight, don't start dieting; change your lifestyle.

---

Today, write down your thoughts on the wisdom of being moderate.

_____

_____

_____

_____

_____

_____

# DAY 13

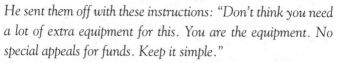

## A SIMPLE FORMULA FOR
## LOSING WEIGHT

*He sent them off with these instructions: "Don't think you need
a lot of extra equipment for this. You are the equipment. No
special appeals for funds. Keep it simple."*

Mark 6:8 MSG

---

Your current weight is the result of the number of calories
that you have taken into your body versus the number of
calories that you have burned. If you seek to lower your
weight, then you must burn more calories (by engaging in
more vigorous physical activities), or take in fewer calories
(by eating more sensibly), or both. It's as simple as that.

---

Write down your estimate of the number of calories that
you consume on an average day. Then, throughout the day.
count the calories you actually consume. Finally, compare
your original estimate to the actual calorie count.

---

_____

_____

_____

_____

_____

_____

_____

# DAY 14

## THE RIGHT KIND OF EXERCISE FOR YOU

*He gives strength to the weary and strengthens the powerless.*

Isaiah 40:29 HCSB

If you want to attain and maintain a healthy lifestyle, it's important to engage in a consistent exercise program. Implementing a plan of regular, sensible exercise is one way of ensuring that you've done your part to care for the body that God has given you. So what's the right kind of exercise for you? That's a question for you and your doctor. But whether you're running marathons or walking around the block, it's important to stay as active as you can, as long as you can. No one can force you to exercise; you'll need to make that decision on your own. And if you genuinely desire to please God, it's a decision that you will make today.

In the space below, write down a few of the benefits that you will enjoy if you exercise regularly.

_____

_____

_____

_____

_____

_____

# DAY 15

## FAITH AND FITNESS

*Cast your burden on the Lord, and He shall sustain you; He shall never permit the righteous to be moved.*

Psalm 55:22 NKJV

---

Faith and fitness. These two words may see disconnected, but they are not. If you're about to begin a regimen of vigorous physical exercise, then you will find it helpful to begin a regimen of vigorous spiritual exercise, too. Why? Because the physical, emotional, and spiritual aspects of your life are interconnected. In other words, you cannot "compartmentalize" physical fitness in one category of your being and spiritual fitness in another—every facet of your life has an impact on the person you are today and the person you will become tomorrow.

---

In the space below, write down a few thoughts about the role that faith plays in your life.

_____

_____

_____

_____

_____

_____

_____

## CHOOSING HEALTHIER FOODS

*For whatever is born of God overcomes the world. And this is the victory that has overcome the world—our faith.*

1 John 5:4 NKJV

Poor eating habits are easy to make and hard to break, but break them you must. Otherwise, you'll be disobeying God's commandments while causing yourselves great harm.

Maintaining a healthy lifestyle is a journey, not a destination, and that journey requires discipline. But rest assured that if you and your loved ones are willing to make the step-by-step journey toward a healthier diet, God is taking careful note of your progress . . . and He's quietly urging you to take the next step.

Today, write down at least three healthy foods that you're going to add to your diet.

_____

_____

_____

_____

_____

_____

_____

# DAY 17

## A LOVE THAT CHANGES EVERYTHING

*Your old life is dead. Your new life, which is your real life—even though invisible to spectators—is with Christ in God. He is your life.*

Colossians 3:3 MSG

Christ's love is perfect and steadfast. Even though we are fallible, and wayward, the Good Shepherd cares for us still. Even though we have fallen far short of the Father's commandments, Christ loves us with a power and depth that is beyond our understanding. And, as we accept Christ's love and walk in Christ's footsteps, our lives bear testimony to His power and to His grace. Yes, Christ's love changes everything; may we invite Him into our hearts so it can then change everything in us.

Write down a few thoughts about your response to Christ's love.

_____

_____

_____

_____

_____

_____

# A DISCIPLINED LIFESTYLE PAYS BIG DIVIDENDS

*Folly is loud; she is undisciplined and without knowledge.*

Proverbs 9:13 NIV

God's Word reminds us again and again that our Creator expects us to be disciplined in our thoughts and disciplined in our actions. God doesn't reward laziness, misbehavior, apathy, or shortsightedness. To the contrary, He expects believers to behave with dignity and self-control. We live in a world in which leisure is glorified and consumption is commercialized. But God has other plans. He did not create us for lives of gluttony or sloth; He created us for far greater things.

High blood pressure can cause heart attacks, strokes, and plenty of other serious health problems. The good news is that high blood pressure is usually treatable. Today, make the effort to take an accurate reading of your blood pressure, and write it in the space below. And if your blood pressure appears to be high, talk to your physician.

## FOLLOWING HIS FOOTSTEPS

*"Follow Me," Jesus told them, "and I will make you into fishers of men!" Immediately they left their nets and followed Him.*

Mark 1:17-18 HCSB

Jesus walks with you. Are you walking with Him? Hopefully, you will choose to walk with Him today and every day of your life. Jesus loved you so much that He endured unspeakable humiliation and suffering for you. How will you respond to Christ's sacrifice? Will you take up His cross and follow Him, or will you choose another path? When you place your hopes squarely at the foot of the cross, when you place Jesus squarely at the center of your life, you will be blessed.

Today, jot down your thoughts on ways that your spiritual, emotional, and physical health are interconnected.

_____

_____

_____

_____

_____

_____

_____

## SAY NO TO UNHEALTHY FOODS

*Dear friend, I pray that you may prosper in every way and be in good health, just as your soul prospers.*

3 John 1:2 HCSB

Do you dine out often? If so, be careful. Most restaurants stay in business by serving big portions of tasty food. Unfortunately, most restaurant food is high in calories, sugar, and fat. You will probably eat healthier meals if you prepare those meals at home instead of eating out.

Today, write down a few of the foods that you should probably eliminate from your diet.

_____

_____

_____

_____

_____

_____

_____

_____

_____

_____

# DAY 21

## IF NOT NOW, WHEN?

*Therefore, get your minds ready for action, being self-disciplined, and set your hope completely on the grace to be brought to you at the revelation of Jesus Christ.*

1 Peter 1:13 HCSB

If you're determined to improve the state of your physical, spiritual, or emotional health, the best time to begin is now. But if you're like most people, you'll be tempted to put things off. The habit of putting things off until the last minute, or the habit of making excuses for work that was never done, can be detrimental to your life, to your character, and to your health. One way that you can learn to defeat procrastination is by paying less attention to the sacrifices you're making today and more attention to the rewards you'll receive tomorrow.

In the space below, write down the most important steps you can take to improve your health today.

_____

_____

_____

_____

_____

_____

## ASKING FOR GOD'S HELP

*So I say to you, ask, and it will be given to you; seek, and you will find; knock, and it will be opened to you. For everyone who asks receives, and he who seeks finds, and to him who knocks it will be opened.*

Luke 11:9-10 NKJV

Do you genuinely want to strengthen your fitness and your faith? If the answer to that question is yes, then you should set aside ample time each morning to ask for God's help. When you do, God will shower you with His blessings, His grace, and His love.

In the space below, write down your thoughts about the power of prayer.

_____

_____

_____

_____

_____

_____

_____

_____

# DAY 23

## MAKING FITNESS FUN

*You will show me the path of life; in Your presence is fullness of joy; at Your right hand are pleasures forevermore.*

Psalm 16:11 NKJV

Your attitude toward exercise is important. If you view it as a form of punishment, you'll exercise less. But, if you can find ways to make exercise fun, you'll be far more likely to achieve your goals. So, if you genuinely want to exercise more, find exercise that you enjoy. And if you can't seem to find exercise that you enjoy, search for ways to make your current exercise program a little less painful and a little more fun.

In the space below, write down several forms of exercise that you enjoy.

_____

_____

_____

_____

_____

_____

_____

## UNBENDING TRUTH

*And put on the new self, which in the likeness of God has been created in righteousness and holiness of the truth. Therefore, laying aside falsehood, speak truth, each one of you, with his neighbor, for we are members of one another.*

Ephesians 4:24-25 NASB

It has been said that character is what we are when nobody is watching. How true. When we do things that we know aren't right, we try to hide them from our families and friends. But even then, God is watching.

If you'd like to improve the quality of your life, your health, or just about anything else, for that matter, be totally honest with others and totally honest with yourself.

In the space below, write down your thoughts about the importance of being totally honest with yourself and with others.

_____

_____

_____

_____

_____

_____

_____

## SOLVING PROBLEMS

*People who do what is right may have many problems, but the Lord will solve them all.*

Psalm 34:19 NCV

When it comes to solving the problems of everyday living, we often know precisely what needs to be done, but we may be slow in doing it—especially if what needs to be done is difficult or uncomfortable for us. So we put off till tomorrow what should be done today. The words of Psalm 34 remind us that the Lord solves problems for "people who do what is right." And usually, doing "what is right" means doing the uncomfortable work of confronting our problems sooner rather than later.

In the space below, write down the most important problem that you need to solve today.

## IT TAKES DISCIPLINE

*Apply your heart to discipline and your ears to words of knowledge.*

Proverbs 23:12 NASB

Physical fitness requires discipline: the discipline to exercise regularly and the discipline to eat sensibly—it's as simple as that. But here's the catch: understanding the need for discipline is easy, but leading a disciplined life can be hard for most of us. Why? Because it's usually more fun to eat a second piece of cake than it is to jog a second lap around the track. Life's greatest rewards usually require lots of work, which is perfectly fine with God. After all, He knows that we're up to the task, and He has big plans for us.

In the space below, ask God to help you find the strength and discipline to meet your goals.

_____

_____

_____

_____

_____

_____

_____

## FITNESS IS A FORM OF WORSHIP

*Worship the Lord your God and . . . serve Him only.*

Matthew 4:10 HCSB

What does worship have to do with fitness? That depends on how you define worship. If you consider worship to be a "Sunday-only" activity, an activity that occurs only inside the four walls of your local church, then fitness and worship may seem totally unrelated. But, if you view worship as an activity that impacts every facet of your life—if you consider worship to be something far more than a "one-day-a week" obligation—then you understand that every aspect of your life is a form of worship. And that includes keeping your body physically fit.

In the space below, write down your thoughts about the rewards you earn by staying physically fit.

_____

_____

_____

_____

_____

_____

_____

## ENTHUSIASTIC DISCIPLESHIP

*Don't work only while being watched, in order to please men, but as slaves of Christ, do God's will from your heart. Render service with a good attitude, as to the Lord and not to men.*

Ephesians 6:6-7 HCSB

With whom will you choose to walk today? Will you walk with shortsighted people who honor the ways of the world, or will you walk with the Son of God? Hopefully, you will choose to walk with Jesus today and every day of your life. Jesus doesn't want you to be a run-of-the-mill, follow-the-crowd kind of person. Jesus wants you to be a "new creation" through Him. And that's exactly what you should want for yourself, too. Jesus deserves your extreme enthusiasm; the world deserves it; and you deserve the experience of sharing it.

In the space below, write down at least one thing you can do today to become a better disciple of Christ.

_____

_____

_____

_____

_____

_____

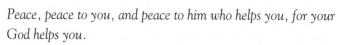

## BEYOND THOSE TEMPORARY SETBACKS

*Peace, peace to you, and peace to him who helps you, for your God helps you.*

1 Chronicles 12:18 HCSB

If you're on a new health regimen, you may relapse back into your old, unhealthy habits. If so, don't waste time or energy beating yourself up. If you've "fallen off the wagon," simply pick yourself up, dust yourself off, and get back on it. God was with you when you were riding that wagon the first time, He was with you when you fell, and He'll welcome you back on the wagon when you're wise enough to climb back on.

In the space below, jot down healthy ways you can reward yourself for doing a good job and not falling off the wagon.

_____

_____

_____

_____

_____

_____

_____

## RECHARGING THE BATTERY

*Come to Me, all you who labor and are heavy laden, and I will give you rest. Take My yoke upon you and learn from Me, for I am gentle and lowly in heart, and you will find rest for your souls. For My yoke is easy and My burden is light.*

Matthew 11:28-30 NKJV

God expects us to work hard, but He also intends for us to rest. When we fail to take the rest that we need, we do a disservice to ourselves and to our families.

Is your spiritual battery running low? Is your energy on the wane? Are your emotions frayed? If so, it's time to turn your thoughts and your prayers to God. And when you're finished, it's time to rest.

In the space below, write down ways that more rest might improve your spiritual, emotional, or physical health.

_____

_____

_____

_____

_____

_____

_____

_____

# YOUR BODY, YOUR CHOICES

*So then each of us shall give account of himself to God.*

Romans 14:12 NKJV

As adults, each of us bears a personal responsibility for the general state of our own physical health. Certainly, various aspects of health are beyond our control: illness sometimes strikes even the healthiest men and women. But for most of us, physical health is a choice: it is the result of hundreds of small decisions that we make every day of our lives. If we make decisions that promote good health, our bodies respond. But if we fall into bad habits and undisciplined lifestyles, we suffer unfortunate consequences. Today, you will make many choices concerning your faith and your fitness. Choose wisely.

In the space below, make a note to yourself and take responsibility for the body God has given you.

_____

_____

_____

_____

_____

_____

## GOD'S PROTECTION

*The Lord is my strength and my song; He has become my salvation.*

Exodus 15:2 HCSB

In a world filled with dangers and temptations, God is the ultimate armor. In a world filled with misleading messages, God's Word is the ultimate truth. In a world filled with more frustrations than we can count, God's Son offers the ultimate peace. Will you accept God's peace and wear God's armor against the dangers of our world?

In the space below, thank God for the times He has protected you in the past. Then ask for His protection today.

_____

_____

_____

_____

_____

_____

_____

_____

_____

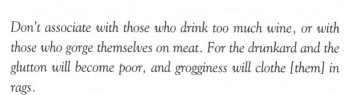

## MODERATION LEADS TO ABUNDANCE

*Don't associate with those who drink too much wine, or with those who gorge themselves on meat. For the drunkard and the glutton will become poor, and grogginess will clothe [them] in rags.*

Proverbs 23:20-21 HCSB

If you sincerely seek the abundant life that Christ has promised, you must learn to control your appetites before they control you. Good habits, like bad ones, are habit-forming. The sooner you acquire the habit of moderation, the better your chances for a long, happy, abundant life.

Today, write down at least one step you can take to become a more moderate person.

_____

_____

_____

_____

_____

_____

_____

_____

## FINDING FULFILLMENT

*For You, O God, have tested us; You have refined us as silver is refined . . . we went through fire and through water; but You brought us out to rich fulfillment.*

Psalm 66:10–12 NKJV

Everywhere we turn, or so it seems, the world promises fulfillment, contentment, and happiness. But the contentment that the world offers is fleeting and incomplete. Thankfully, the fulfillment that God offers is all encompassing and everlasting. Sometimes, amid the inevitable hustle and bustle of life, we can forfeit—albeit temporarily—the joy of Christ as we wrestle with the challenges of daily living. Yet God's Word is clear: fulfillment through Christ is available to all who seek it and claim it. Your task is to claim His abundance today.

In the space below, write down your thoughts about experiencing genuine peace through Jesus.

_____

_____

_____

_____

_____

_____

## A TERRIFIC TOMORROW

*"For I know the plans I have for you"—[this is] the Lord's declaration—"plans for [your] welfare, not for disaster, to give you a future and a hope."*

Jeremiah 29:11 HCSB

The way that you think about your future will play a powerful role in determining how things turn out (it's called the "self-fulfilling prophecy," and it applies to everybody, including you). Are you expecting a terrific tomorrow, or are you dreading a terrible one? The answer to that question will have a powerful impact on the way tomorrow unfolds. Today, as you live in the present and look to the future, remember that God has an amazing plan for you. Act—and believe—accordingly.

In the space below, write down your thoughts about the eternally bright future that can be yours through Jesus.

_____

_____

_____

_____

_____

_____

## LISTENING TO GOD

*The one who is from God listens to God's words. This is why you don't listen, because you are not from God.*

John 8:47 HCSB

Sometimes God speaks loudly and clearly. More often, He speaks in a quiet voice—and if you are wise, you will be listening carefully when He does. To do so, you must carve out quiet moments each day to study His Word and sense His direction. Can you quiet yourself long enough to listen to your conscience? Are you attuned to the subtle guidance of your intuition? Are you willing to pray sincerely and then to wait quietly for God's response? Hopefully so. If you sincerely desire to hear His voice, you must listen carefully, and you must do so in the silent corners of your quiet, willing heart.

Today, be quiet and still. Then, in the silence, write down at least one thing you think God is trying to tell you.

_____

_____

_____

_____

_____

_____

## IN FOCUS

*Look straight ahead, and fix your eyes on what lies before you. Mark out a straight path for your feet; then stick to the path and stay safe. Don't get sidetracked; keep your feet from following evil.*

Proverbs 4:25-27 NLT

What is your focus today? Are you willing to focus your thoughts and energies on God's blessings and upon His will for your life? Or will you turn your thoughts to other things? This day—and every day hereafter—is a chance to celebrate the life that God has given you. It's also a chance to give thanks to the One who has offered you more blessings than you can possibly count.

Fill the space below with just a few of the many blessings God has given you.

## EXTREME CHANGES

*Then He said to them all, "If anyone wants to come with Me,
he must deny himself, take up his cross daily, and follow Me."*

Luke 9:23 HCSB

Nothing is more important than your wholehearted commitment to your Creator and to His only begotten Son.
Your faith must never be an afterthought; it must be your
ultimate priority, your ultimate possession, and your ultimate passion. You are the recipient of Christ's love. Accept it enthusiastically and share it passionately. Jesus deserves your extreme enthusiasm; the world deserves it; and
you deserve the experience of sharing it.

In the space below, write down your thoughts about your
relationship with Jesus.

_____

_____

_____

_____

_____

_____

_____

## A PASSION FOR LIFE

*But those who trust in the Lord will renew their strength; they will soar on wings like eagles; they will run and not grow weary; they will walk and not faint.*

Isaiah 40:31 HCSB

Are you enthused about life, or do you struggle through each day giving scarcely a thought to God's blessings? Are you constantly praising God for His gifts, and are you sharing His Good News with the world? You should be. You are the recipient of Christ's sacrificial love. Accept it enthusiastically and share it fervently. Jesus deserves your enthusiasm; the world deserves it; and you deserve the experience of sharing it.

In the space below, make a few notes about your priorities. Are you really putting God first in your life, or are you putting other things ahead of your relationship with the Father?

_____

_____

_____

_____

_____

_____

# DAY 40

## FOOD MATTERS

*Do not carouse with drunkards and gluttons, for they are on their way to poverty.*

Proverbs 23:20-21 NLT

---

Many of us are remarkably ill-informed and amazingly apathetic about the foods we eat. We feast on high-fat fast foods. We swoon over sweets. We order up—and promptly pack away—prodigious portions. The result is a society in which too many of us become the human equivalents of the portions we purchase: oversized. A healthier strategy, of course, is to pay more attention to the nutritional properties of our foods and less attention to their taste.

---

Today, make a few notes about the quality and the quantity of the foods you eat.

_____

_____

_____

_____

_____

_____

_____

# DAY 41

## REGULAR EXERCISE PAYS BIG DIVIDENDS

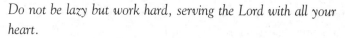

*Do not be lazy but work hard, serving the Lord with all your heart.*

Romans 12:11 NCV

The benefits of exercise are both physical and emotional. But no one can exercise for you; it's up to you to exercise, or not. Your exercise regimen should be sensible, enjoyable, safe, and consistent.

Today, write about your exercise regimen. List what you do on a regular basis and some of the ways you could improve the future.

_____

_____

_____

_____

_____

_____

_____

_____

_____

## MOVING MOUNTAINS

*If you have faith as a mustard seed, you will say to this mountain, "Move from here to there," and it will move; and nothing will be impossible for you.*

Matthew 17:20 NKJV

---

Every life—including yours—is a series of successes and failures, celebrations and disappointments, joys and sorrows. Every step of the way, through every triumph and tragedy, God will stand by your side and strengthen you . . . if you have faith in Him. Jesus taught His disciples that if they had faith, they could move mountains. You can too.

---

In the space below, make a list of the mountains you need to move. Then, ask God to help you move them.

_____

_____

_____

_____

_____

_____

_____

_____

# DAY 43

## BEYOND BITTERNESS

*All bitterness, anger and wrath, insult and slander must be removed from you, along with all wickedness. And be kind and compassionate to one another, forgiving one another, just as God also forgave you in Christ.*

Ephesians 4:31-32 HCSB

Bitterness is a stress-inducing spiritual sickness. It will consume your soul; it is dangerous to your emotional health. It can destroy you if you let it . . . so don't let it! How can you rid yourself of these feelings? First, you must prayerfully ask God to cleanse your heart. Then, you must learn to catch yourself whenever thoughts of bitterness or hatred begin to attack you. Your challenge is this: You must learn to resist negative thoughts before they hijack your emotions.

In the space below, make a list of people you need to forgive or things you need to forget.

_____

_____

_____

_____

_____

_____

## SO MANY TEMPTATIONS

*Don't you know that you are God's sanctuary and that the Spirit of God lives in you?*

1 Corinthians 3:16 HCSB

Our world is teeming with temptations and distractions that can rob you of the physical, emotional, and spiritual fitness that might otherwise be yours. And if you're not careful, the struggles and stresses of everyday living can rob you of the peace that should rightfully be yours because of your personal relationship with Christ. So take time each day to have a personal training session with your Savior. Don't be a person who's satisfied with occasional visits to church on Sunday morning. Instead, build a relationship with Jesus that deepens day by day.

In the space below, write down your thoughts about the ways that your spiritual health impacts your physical health, and vice-versa.

_____

_____

_____

_____

_____

_____

## MAKING THE RIGHT CHOICES

*A wise man will hear and increase learning, and a man of understanding will attain wise counsel.*

Proverbs 1:5 NKJV

John Maxwell observed, "The key to healthy eating is moderation and managing what you eat every day." And he was right. Crash diets don't usually work, but sensible eating habits do work, so plan your meals accordingly.

Today, write about some of the unwise choices you've made in the past and then write about the wise choices you intend to make in the future.

_____

_____

_____

_____

_____

_____

_____

_____

_____

_____

## DO FIRST THINGS FIRST

*Therefore, get your minds ready for action, being self-disciplined . . . .*

1 Peter 1:13 HCSB

"First things first." These words are easy to speak but hard to put into practice. If you're having trouble prioritizing your day, perhaps you've been trying to organize your life according to your own plans, not God's. A better strategy, of course, is to take your daily obligations and place them in the hands of the One who created you. To do so, you must prioritize your day according to God's commandments, and you must seek His will and His wisdom in all matters, including matters of faith and fitness.

When it comes to food, fitness, or faith, the best moment to begin major improvements is the present moment. In the space below, jot down something you can do to improve your health today.

---

---

---

---

---

## FORGIVING AND FORGETTING

*But the wisdom from above is first pure, then peace-loving, gentle, compliant, full of mercy and good fruits, without favoritism and hypocrisy.*

James 3:17 HCSB

Do you have a tough time forgiving and forgetting? If so, welcome to the club. Most of us find it difficult to forgive the people who have hurt us. And that's too bad because life would be much simpler if we could forgive people "once and for all" and be done with it. Yet forgiveness is seldom that easy. Usually, the decision to forgive is straightforward, but the process of forgiving is more difficult. Forgiveness is a journey that requires time, perseverance, and prayer. Don't expect forgiveness to be easy or quick, but rest assured: with God as your partner, you can forgive.

Today, write a list of the people you have forgiven from the list a few days ago (hopefully you're on this list, too).

_____

_____

_____

_____

_____

_____

## YOU ARE BLESSED

*I will make them and the area around My hill a blessing: I will send down showers in their season—showers of blessing.*

Ezekiel 34:26 HCSB

If you sat down and began counting your blessings, how long would it take? A very, very long time! Your blessings include life, freedom, family, friends, talents, and possessions, for starters. But, your greatest blessing—a gift that is yours for the asking—is God's gift of salvation through Christ Jesus.

Today, begin making a list of your blessings. You most certainly will not be able to make a complete list, but take a few moments and jot down as many blessings as you can. Then give thanks to the giver of all good things: God. His love for you is eternal, as are His gifts. And it's never too soon—or too late—to offer Him thanks.

# DAY 49

## BORN AGAIN

*You have been born again—not of perishable seed but of imperishable—through the living and enduring word of God.*

1 Peter 1:23 HCSB

Why did Christ die on the cross? Christ sacrificed His life so that we might be born again. This gift, freely given from God's only begotten Son, is the priceless possession of everyone who accepts Him as Lord and Savior. Let us claim Christ's gift today. Let us walk with the Savior, let us love Him, let us praise Him, and let us share His message of salvation with all those who cross our paths. The comforting words of Ephesians 2:8 make God's promise clear: "For by grace you have been saved through faith, and that not of yourselves; it is the gift of God" (NKJV). Thus, we are saved not because of our good deeds but because of our faith in Christ.

In the space below, write down a few thoughts about Christ's astounding gift: the gift of eternal life.

## START MAKING CHANGES NOW

*But be doers of the word and not hearers only.*

James 1:22 HCSB

Warren Wiersbe correctly observed, "A Christian should no more defile his body than a Jew would defile the temple." Unfortunately, too many of us have allowed our temples to fall into disrepair. When it comes to fitness and food, it's easy to fall into bad habits. And it's easy to convince ourselves that we'll start improving our health "some day." But, if we are to care for our bodies in the way that God intends, we must establish healthy habits, and we must establish them sooner rather than later.

Today, pick out one important obligation that you've been putting off. Then, take at least one specific step toward the completion of the task you've been avoiding. Even if you don't finish the job, you'll discover that it's easier to finish a job that you've already begun than to finish a job that you've never started.

_____

_____

_____

_____

_____

# DAY 51

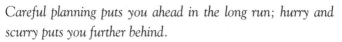

## TOO BUSY?

*Careful planning puts you ahead in the long run; hurry and scurry puts you further behind.*

Proverbs 21:5 MSG

Are you making time each day to praise God and to study His Word? If so, you know firsthand the blessings that He offers those who worship Him consistently and sincerely. But, if you have unintentionally allowed the hustle and bustle of your busy day to come between you and your Creator, then you must slow down, take a deep breath, and rearrange your priorities. God loved this world so much that He sent His Son to save it. And now only one real question remains for you: what will you do in response to God's love? The answer should be obvious: God must come first in your life.

The world wants to grab every spare minute of your time, but God wants some of your time, too. In the space below, write down a few of the rewards you receive when you spend time with God.

_____

_____

_____

_____

## THIS IS HIS DAY

*This is the day the Lord has made; let us rejoice and be glad in it.*

Psalm 118:24 HCSB

---

The 118th Psalm reminds us that today, like every other day, is a cause for celebration. Today is a non-renewable resource—once it's gone, it's gone forever. It's up to you to treasure the time that God has given you. So give Him the glory and the praise and the thanksgiving that He deserves. And search for the hidden possibilities that God has placed along your path. This day is a priceless gift from the Creator, so use it joyfully and encourage others to do likewise. After all, this is the day the Lord has made....

---

In the space below, thank your Creator for the gift of life.

_____

_____

_____

_____

_____

_____

_____

## TRUST HIS GUIDANCE

*And he said: "The Lord is my rock and my fortress and my deliverer; the God of my strength, in whom I will trust."*

2 Samuel 22:2-3 NKJV

---

The cure for obesity is simple, but implementing that cure isn't. Weight loss requires lots of planning and lots of self-discipline. But with God's help, you're up to the task. When you have challenges of any kind, God stands ready to guide you. Your responsibility, of course, is to ask Him for guidance about food, fitness, faith, and life.

---

In the space below, ask God to lead you to a place of spiritual, emotional, and physical health.

_____

_____

_____

_____

_____

_____

_____

_____

_____

## SUPPORTING HIS CHURCH

*For we are God's fellow workers; you are God's field, you are God's building.*

1 Corinthians 3:9 NKJV

---

The church belongs to God; it is His just as certainly as we are His. When we help build God's church, we bear witness to the changes that He has made in our lives. Today and every day, let us worship God with grateful hearts and helping hands as we support the church that He has created. Let us witness to our friends, to our families, and to the world. When we do so, we bless others—and we are blessed by the One who sent His Son to die so that we might have eternal life.

---

In the space below, write down your thoughts about ways you can make church a celebration.

_____

_____

_____

_____

_____

_____

_____

## COMPASSIONATE SERVANTS

*Finally, all of you be of one mind, having compassion for one another; love as brothers, be tenderhearted, be courteous.*

1 Peter 3:8 NKJV

As believers, we have been richly blessed by our Creator. We, in turn, are called to share our gifts, our possessions, our testimonies, and our talents. Concentration camp survivor Corrie ten Boom correctly observed, "The measure of a life is not its duration but its donation." These words remind us that the quality of our lives is determined not by what are able to take from others, but instead by what we are able to share with others. The thread of compassion is woven into the very fabric of Christ's teachings. If we are to be disciples of Christ, we, too, must be zealous in caring for others. Our Savior expects no less from us. And He deserves no less.

In the space below, write down at least three people who need your help today.

_____

_____

_____

_____

_____

## NO COMPLAINTS

*Do everything without grumbling and arguing, so that you may be blameless and pure.*

Philippians 2:14-15 HCSB

---

Because we are imperfect human beings, we often lose sight of our blessings. Ironically, most of us have more blessings than we can count, but we may still find reasons to complain about the minor frustrations of everyday life. To do so, of course, is not only wrong; it is also the pinnacle of shortsightedness and a serious roadblock on the path to spiritual abundance. Are you tempted to complain about the inevitable minor frustrations of everyday living? Don't do it! Today and every day, make it a practice to count your blessings, not your hardships. It's the truly decent way to live.

---

If you're wise, you'll fill your heart with gratitude. When you do, there's simply no room left for complaints. In the space below, write down several things you're thankful for.

_____

_____

_____

_____

_____

## WORKING HARD FOR GOOD HEALTH

*Work brings profit, but mere talk leads to poverty!*

Proverbs 14:23 NLT

Life is a gift—health must be earned. We earn good health by cultivating healthy habits. This is the right time for you to commit yourself to a more sensible lifestyle. So take a close look at your habits: how you eat, how you exercise, and how you think about your health. The only way that you'll revolutionize your physical health is to revolutionize the habits that make up the fabric of your day.

In the space below, write down something you can do today to improve your faith or your fitness.

_____

_____

_____

_____

_____

_____

_____

_____

_____

# REAL TRANSFORMATION?
# INNER TRANSFORMATION!

*Therefore if anyone is in Christ, he is a new creature; the old things passed away; behold, new things have come.*

2 Corinthians 5:17 HCSB

---

When you invited Christ to reign over your heart, you became a new creation through Him. This day offers yet another opportunity to behave yourself like that new creation by serving your Creator and strengthening your faith. When you do, God will guide your steps and bless your endeavors today and forever.

---

Today, if you're serious about improving your physical and spiritual health, write down a brief prayer about faith and fitness.

_____

_____

_____

_____

_____

_____

_____

## GOOD WORKS NOW, NOT LATER

*This is how we are sure that we have come to know Him: by keeping His commands.*

1 John 2:3 HCSB

---

When we seek righteousness in our own lives—and when we seek the companionship of those who do likewise—we reap the spiritual rewards that God intends for us to enjoy. Today, as you fulfill your responsibilities, hold fast to that which is good, and associate yourself with believers who behave themselves in like fashion. When you do, your good works will serve as a powerful example for others and as a worthy offering to your Creator.

---

In the space below, write down at least one good deed you're going to do today.

---

---

---

---

---

---

---

# BELIEVING MAKES A DIFFERENCE

*You love Him, though you have not seen Him. And though not seeing Him now, you believe in Him and rejoice with inexpressible and glorious joy, because you are receiving the goal of your faith, the salvation of your souls.*

1 Peter 1:8-9 HCSB

If you'd like to partake in the peace that only God can give, make certain that your actions are guided by His Word. And while you're at it, pay careful attention to the conscience that God, in His infinite wisdom, has placed in your heart. Don't treat your faith as if it were separate from your everyday life. Weave your beliefs about physical and spiritual matters into the very fabric of your day. When you do, God will honor your good works, and your good works will honor God.

Doing God's work is a responsibility that every Christian (including you) should bear. In the space below, write down at least one good work that you will do today.

_____

_____

_____

_____

_____

## THE GIFT OF CHEERFULNESS

*Worry is a heavy load, but a kind word cheers you up.*

Proverbs 12:25 NCV

Cheerfulness is a healthy, life-altering gift that we give to others and to ourselves. And, as believers who have been saved by a risen Christ, why shouldn't we be cheerful? The answer, of course, is that we have every reason to honor our Savior with joy in our hearts, smiles on our faces, and words of celebration on our lips.

In the space below, write down your thoughts about the rewards of cheerfulness.

_____

_____

_____

_____

_____

_____

_____

_____

_____

_____

## THE FUTILITY OF BLAME

*People's own foolishness ruins their lives, but in their minds they blame the Lord.*

Proverbs 19:3 NCV

When our unhealthy habits lead to poor health, we find it all too easy to look beyond ourselves and assign blame. In fact, we live in a society where blame has become a national obsession: we blame cigarette manufacturers, restaurants, and food producers, to name only a few. But to blame others is to miss the point: we, and we alone, are responsible for the way that we treat our bodies. And the sooner that we accept that responsibility, the sooner we can assert control over our bodies and our lives. So, when it comes to your own body, assume control and accept responsibility. It's a great way to live and a great way to stay healthy.

Today, write down your thoughts about the need to take responsibility for the current state of your health.

_____

_____

_____

_____

_____

# DAY 63

## PRAY CONSTANTLY ABOUT EVERYTHING, INCLUDING YOUR HEALTH

*Rejoice always! Pray constantly. Give thanks in everything, for this is God's will for you in Christ Jesus.*

1 Thessalonians 5:16-18 HCSB

Theologian Wayne Oates once admitted, "Many of my prayers are made with my eyes open. You see, it seems I'm always praying about something, and it's not always convenient—or safe—to close my eyes." Dr. Oates understood that God always hears our prayers and that the relative position of our eyelids is of no concern to Him. Today, find a little more time to lift your concerns to God in prayer and praise. Pray about everything, including your spiritual and physical health.

Today, write down a few of your thoughts about the power of constant prayer and the role that prayer plays in your life.

_____

_____

_____

_____

_____

## THE BATTLE IS WON

*Cast your burden on the Lord, and He will support you; He will never allow the righteous to be shaken.*

Psalm 55:22 HCSB

Christians have every reason to live courageously. After all, the ultimate battle has already been won on the cross at Calvary. When you find yourself worried about the challenges of today or the uncertainties of tomorrow, you must ask yourself whether or not you are ready to place your concerns and your life in God's all-powerful, all-knowing, all-loving hands. If the answer to that question is yes—as it should be—then you can draw courage today from the source of strength that never fails: your Heavenly Father.

In the space below, write down at least one burden that you should "cast upon the Lord" today.

_____

_____

_____

_____

_____

_____

_____

## CRITICS BEWARE

*Don't pick on people, jump on their failures, criticize their faults—unless, of course, you want the same treatment. Don't condemn those who are down; that hardness can boomerang. Be easy on people; you'll find life a lot easier.*

Luke 6:37 MSG

From experience, we know that it is easier to criticize than to correct. And we know that it is easier to find faults than solutions. Yet the urge to criticize others remains a powerful temptation for most of us. Our task, as obedient believers, is to break the twin habits of negative thinking and critical speech. Negativity is highly contagious: we give it to others who, in turn, give it back to us. This cycle can be broken by positive thoughts, heartfelt prayers, and encouraging words. As thoughtful servants of a loving God, we can use the transforming power of Christ's love to break the chains of negativity. And we should.

In the space below, write down your thoughts about the rewards of staying positive and the costs of being negative.

_____

_____

_____

_____

_____

## HEALTHY PRIORITIES

*Beloved, I pray that in all respects you may prosper and be in good health, just as your soul prospers.*

3 John 1:2 NASB

When it comes to matters concerning health—whether physical, emotional, or spiritual fitness—God's Word can help us establish clear priorities that can guide our steps and our lives. If you're having trouble prioritizing your day—or if you're having trouble sticking to a plan that enhances your spiritual and physical health—perhaps you've been trying to organize your life according to your own plans, not God's. A better strategy, of course, is to take your daily obligations and place them in the hands of the One who created you. To do so, you must prioritize your day according to God's commandments, and you must seek His will and His wisdom in all matters.

In the space below, write down your thoughts about the rewards of a healthy lifestyle.

_____

_____

_____

_____

_____

_____

# THE GUIDEBOOK

*There's nothing like the written Word of God for showing you the way to salvation through faith in Christ Jesus. Every part of Scripture is God-breathed and useful one way or another, showing us truth, exposing our rebellion, correcting our mistakes, training us to live God's way. Through the Word we are put together and shaped up for the tasks God has for us.*

2 Timothy 3:15-17 MSG

When it comes to matters of physical, spiritual, and emotional health, Christians possess an infallible guidebook: the Holy Bible. The Creator has given us the Bible for the purpose of knowing His promises, His power, His commandments, His wisdom, His love, and His Son. As we study God's teachings and apply them to our lives, we live by the Word that shall never pass away.

In the space below, thank your Creator for the gift of His Holy Word.

# DAY 68

## A CLEAR CONSCIENCE

*Let us draw near with a true heart in full assurance of faith, our hearts sprinkled clean from an evil conscience and our bodies washed in pure water.*

Few things in life torment us more than a guilty conscience. And, few things in life provide more contentment than the knowledge that we are obeying God's commandments.

A clear conscience is one of the rewards we earn when we obey God's Word and follow His will. When we follow God's will and accept His gift of salvation, our earthly rewards are never-ceasing, and our heavenly rewards are everlasting.

In the space below, write down your thoughts about the rewards of a clear conscience.

_____

_____

_____

_____

_____

_____

_____

## CONTENTMENT THAT LASTS

*A tranquil heart is life to the body, but jealousy is rottenness to the bones.*

Proverbs 14:30 HCSB

The preoccupation with happiness and contentment is an ever-present theme in the modern world. We are bombarded with messages that tell us where to find peace and pleasure in a world that worships materialism and wealth. But, lasting contentment is not found in material possessions; genuine contentment is a spiritual gift from God to those who trust in Him and follow His commandments. When God dwells at the center of our lives, peace and contentment will belong to us just as surely as we belong to God.

In the space below, write down your thoughts about the things that provide lasting contentment for you and your family.

## ADVERSITY BUILDS CHARACTER

*God is our refuge and strength, a very present help in trouble.*

Psalm 46:1 NKJV

Psalm 145 promises, "The Lord is near to all who call on him, to all who call on him in truth. He fulfills the desires of those who fear him; he hears their cry and saves them" (vv. 18-20 NIV). As Christians, we know that God loves us and that He will protect us. In times of hardship, He will comfort us; in times of sorrow, He will dry our tears. When we are troubled, or weak, or sorrowful, God is always with us. We must build our lives on the rock that cannot be shaken: we must trust in God. And then, we must get on with the character-building, life-altering work of tackling our problems . . . because if we don't, who will?

In the space below, write down your thoughts about God's willingness to help you achieve your goals.

_____

_____

_____

_____

_____

_____

_____

## DEFEATING TEMPTATION

*But remember that the temptations that come into your life are no different from what others experience. And God is faithful. He will keep the temptation from becoming so strong that you can't stand up against it. When you are tempted, he will show you a way out so that you will not give in to it.*

1 Corinthians 10:13 NLT

If you're trying to remodel yourself, you'll need to remodel your environment, too. In order to decrease temptations and increase the probability of success, you should take a long, hard look at your home, your office, and the places you frequently visit. Then, you must do whatever you can to move yourself as far as possible from the temptations you intend to defeat.

In the space below, write down at least three things you can do to distance yourself from temptation.

_____

_____

_____

_____

_____

_____

_____

## IT'S UP TO YOU TO ASK

*Now if any of you lacks wisdom, he should ask God, who gives to all generously and without criticizing, and it will be given to him.*

James 1:5 HCSB

Do you have questions about your future that you simply can't answer? Do you have needs that you simply can't meet by yourself? Do you sincerely seek to know God's unfolding plans for your life? If so, ask Him for direction, for protection, and for strength—and then keep asking Him every day that you live. Whatever your need, no matter how great or small, pray about it and never lose hope. God is not just near; He is here, and He's perfectly capable of answering your prayers. Now, it's up to you to ask.

If you're searching for peace and abundance, ask for God's help—and keep asking—until He answers your prayers. Today, write down a specific need and pray about it.

_____

_____

_____

_____

_____

_____

## FACING FEARS, LIVING BOLDLY

*For God has not given us a spirit of fearfulness, but one of power, love, and sound judgment.*

2 Timothy 1:7 HCSB

When Paul wrote Timothy, he reminded his young protégé that the God they served was a bold God, and God's Spirit empowered His children with boldness also. Like Timothy, we face times of uncertainty and fear. God's message is the same to us, today, as it was to Timothy: We can live boldly because the spirit of God resides in us. So today, as you face the challenges of everyday living, remember that God is with you . . . and you are protected.

In the space below, write down your thoughts about God's protection.

_____

_____

_____

_____

_____

_____

_____

## YOUR BODY IS IMPORTANT TO GOD

*Don't you know that you are God's sanctuary and that the Spirit of God lives in you?*

1 Corinthians 3:16 HCSB

---

God's Word contains powerful lessons about every aspect of your life, including your health. So, if you're concerned about your spiritual, physical, or emotional health, the first place to turn is that timeless source of comfort and assurance, the Holy Bible. When you open your Bible and begin reading, you'll quickly be reminded of this fact: when you face concerns of any sort—including health-related challenges—God is with you. And His healing touch, like His love, endures forever.

---

It's important to educate yourself on which foods are healthy and which foods aren't. It's important to read labels and learn the basics of proper nutrition. Today, write down five foods that you need to learn more about. Then, take the time to learn about their calorie-count and their nutritional qualities.

_____

_____

_____

_____

_____

## ALWAYS WITH US

*For unto us a Child is born, unto us a Son is given; and the government will be upon His shoulder. And His name will be called Wonderful, Counselor, Mighty God, Everlasting Father, Prince of Peace.*

Isaiah 9:6 NKJV

Are you facing difficult circumstances or unwelcome changes? If so, please remember that God is far bigger than any problem you may face. So, instead of worrying about life's inevitable challenges, put your faith in the Father and His only begotten Son: "Jesus Christ is the same yesterday, today, and forever" (Hebrews 13:8 NKJV). And remember: it is precisely because your Savior does not change that you can face your challenges with courage for today and hope for tomorrow.

In the space below, write down your thoughts about God's promises, God's protection, and God's love.

_____

_____

_____

_____

_____

_____

## CHARACTER-BUILDING TAKES TIME

*The one who lives with integrity will be helped, but one who distorts right and wrong will suddenly fall.*

Proverbs 28:18 HCSB

Character is built slowly over a lifetime. It is the sum of every right decision, every honest word, every noble thought, and every heartfelt prayer. It is forged on the anvil of honorable work and polished by the twin virtues of generosity and humility. Character is a precious thing—difficult to build but easy to tear down. As believers in Christ, we must seek to live each day with discipline, honesty, and faith. When we do, integrity becomes a habit. And God smiles.

In the space below, write down a few of your thoughts about the rewards of honesty.

_____

_____

_____

_____

_____

_____

_____

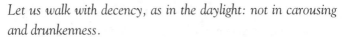

# MISDIRECTED WORSHIP:
# THE TRAGEDY OF ADDICTION

*Let us walk with decency, as in the daylight: not in carousing and drunkenness.*

Romans 13:13 HCSB

The dictionary defines addiction as "the compulsive need for a habit-forming substance; the condition of being habitually and compulsively occupied with something." That definition is accurate, but incomplete. For Christians, addiction has an additional meaning: it means compulsively worshipping something other than God. For the addict, addiction comes first. In the life of an addict, addiction rules. God, of course, commands otherwise. God says, "You shall have no other gods before Me," (Exodus 20:3 NKJV) and He means precisely what He says.

Gerald May observed, "Addiction is the most powerful psychic enemy of humanity's desire for God." In the space below, write down any of your own behaviors that have the potential to become addictive.

_____

_____

_____

_____

_____

## CHOOSING THE GOOD LIFE

*And in that day you will ask Me nothing. Most assuredly, I say to you, whatever you ask the Father in My name He will give you. Until now you have asked nothing in My name. Ask, and you will receive, that your joy may be full.*

John 16:23-24 NKJV

Whether or not we accept God's abundance is, of course, up to each of us. What is your focus today? Are you focused on God's Word and His will for your life? Or are you focused on the distractions and temptations of a difficult world? The answer to this question will, to a surprising extent, determine the quality and the direction of your day. If you sincerely seek the spiritual abundance that your Savior offers, then follow Him completely and without reservation. When you do, you will receive the love, the life, and the abundance that He has promised.

In the space below, write down your thoughts about the abundant life that is available through Christ.

_____

_____

_____

_____

## KEEPING UP APPEARANCES

*We justify our actions by appearances; God examines our motives.*

Proverbs 21:2 MSG

---

The world sees you as you appear to be; God sees you as you really are . . . He sees your heart, and He understands your intentions. The opinions of others should be relatively unimportant to you; however, God's view of you—His understanding of your actions, your thoughts, and your motivations—should be vitally important. Few things in life are more futile than "keeping up appearances" for the sake of neighbors. What is important, of course, is pleasing your Father in heaven. You please Him when your intentions are pure and your actions are just.

---

In the space below, write down your thoughts about the appearances that should really matter to you.

---

---

---

---

---

---

---

# THE POWER OF DAILY WORSHIP AND MEDITATION

*Man shall not live by bread alone, but by every word that proceeds from the mouth of God.*

Matthew 4:4 NKJV

---

Are you concerned about your spiritual, physical, or emotional fitness? If so, there is a timeless source of advice and comfort upon which you can—and should—depend. That source is the Holy Bible.

God has given you the Holy Bible for the purpose of knowing His promises, His power, His commandments, His wisdom, His love, and His Son. As you seek to improve the state of your own health, study God's teachings and apply them to your life. When you do, you will be blessed now and forever.

---

God's Word has the power to change every aspect of your life, including your health. In the space below, write down the benefits you receive when you read God's Word every morning.

---

---

---

---

---

# DAY 81

## HEALTH CAN BE HABIT-FORMING

*Wisdom and strength belong to God; counsel and understanding are His.*

Job 12:13 HCSB

First you make choices, and soon those choices begin to shape your life. That's why you must make smart choices or face the consequences of making dumb ones. Do you think God wants you to develop healthy habits? Of course He does! Physical, emotional, and spiritual fitness are all part of God's plan for you. But it's up to you to make certain that a healthy lifestyle is a fundamental part of your plan, too.

Today, write down at least one new habit that you'd like to acquire.

_____

_____

_____

_____

_____

_____

_____

_____

## DAY 82

## CONQUERING OUR FRUSTRATIONS

*People with quick tempers cause trouble, but those who control their tempers stop a quarrel.*

Proverbs 15:18 NCV

Life is full of frustrations: some great and some small. On occasion, you, like Jesus, will confront evil, and when you do, you may respond as He did: vigorously and without reservation. But, more often your frustrations will be of the more mundane variety. When you are tempted to lose your temper over the minor inconveniences of life, don't. Turn away from anger, hatred, bitterness, and regret. Turn instead to God. When you do, you'll be following His commandments and giving yourself a priceless gift . . . the gift of peace.

In the space below, write down your thoughts about the way you typically deal with feelings of anger or frustration.

_____

_____

_____

_____

_____

_____

_____

## FINDING CONTENTMENT

*I have learned to be content in whatever circumstances I am.*

Philippians 4:11 HCSB

Are you a contented Christian? If so, then you're well aware of the healing power of the risen Christ. But if your spirit is temporarily troubled, perhaps you need to focus less upon your own priorities and more upon God's priorities. When you do, you'll rediscover this life-changing truth: Genuine contentment begins with God . . . and ends there.

Be contented with where you are today, even if it's not exactly where you want to be tomorrow. God has something wonderful in store for you—and remember that God's timing is perfect—so be patient. In the space below, jot down a few of the many blessings that God has given you today.

# KNOW WHAT YOU EAT

*Acquire wisdom—how much better it is than gold! And acquire understanding—it is preferable to silver.*

Proverbs 16:16 HCSB

How hard is it for us to know the nutritional properties of the foods we eat? Not very hard. In the grocery store, almost every food item is clearly marked. In fast-food restaurants, the fat and calorie contents are posted on the wall (although the print is incredibly small, and with good reason: the health properties of these tasty tidbits are, in most cases, so poor that we should rename them "fat foods").

As informed adults, we have access to all the information that we need to make healthy dietary choices. Now it's up to each of us to make wise dietary choices, or not. Those choices are ours, and so are their consequences.

Today, in the space below, make it a point to measure every calorie you consume. Then, at the end of the day, ask yourself if your food choices have been wise, unwise, or disastrous.

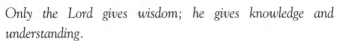

## WISDOM 101

*Only the Lord gives wisdom; he gives knowledge and understanding.*

Proverbs 2:6 NCV

---

If you're looking for wisdom (health or otherwise), the Book of Proverbs is a wonderful place to start. It has 31 chapters, one for each day of the month. If you read Proverbs regularly, and if you take its teachings to heart, you'll gain timeless wisdom from God's unchanging Word.

---

In the space below, write down a few of the most important things that you need to ask God today.

_____

_____

_____

_____

_____

_____

_____

_____

_____

_____

## A LIFE OF ABUNDANCE

*I have come that they may have life, and that they may have it more abundantly.*

John 10:10 NKJV

The 10th chapter of John tells us that Christ came to earth so that our lives might be filled with abundance. Jesus offers His own brand of abundance: a spiritual richness that extends beyond the temporal boundaries of this world. This everlasting abundance is available to all who seek it and claim it. May we, as believers, claim the riches of Christ Jesus every day that we live, and may we share His blessings with all who cross our path.

In the space below, write down your thoughts about Christ's promise of abundant life and what that promise means to you.

_____

_____

_____

_____

_____

_____

_____

# DAY 87

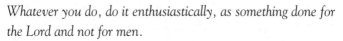

## BE ENTHUSIASTIC

*Whatever you do, do it enthusiastically, as something done for the Lord and not for men.*

Colossians 3:23 HCSB

Are you passionate about your faith, your fitness, and your future? Hopefully so. But if your zest for life has waned, it is now time to redirect your efforts and recharge your spiritual batteries. And that means refocusing your priorities by putting God first. Nothing is more important than your wholehearted commitment to your Creator and to His only begotten Son. Your faith must never be an afterthought; it must be your ultimate priority, your ultimate possession, and your ultimate passion. When you become passionate about your faith, you'll become passionate about your life, too.

In the space below, write down a personal goal that you're excited about. Then, ask God to help you achieve it.

_____

_____

_____

_____

_____

_____

## PROTECTING YOUR
## EMOTIONAL HEALTH

*I will give you a new heart and put a new spirit in you....*

Ezekiel 36:26 NIV

Emotional health isn't simply the absence of sadness; it's also the ability to enjoy life and the wisdom to celebrate God's gifts. Christians have every reason to be optimistic about life. But sometimes, when we are tired or frustrated, rejoicing seems only a distant promise. Thankfully, God stands ready to restore us: our task, of course, is to let Him.

When negative emotions threaten to hijack your day, you should lift your thoughts—and your prayers—to God. In the space below, write down a few of your ideas about the power of prayer.

_____

_____

_____

_____

_____

_____

_____

# SENSIBLE EXERCISE

*No discipline seems pleasant at the time, but painful. Later on, however, it produces a harvest of righteousness and peace for those who have been trained by it.*

Hebrews 12:11 NIV

A healthy lifestyle includes regular, sensible physical exercise. Make no mistake: if you sincerely desire to be a thoughtful caretaker of the body that God has given you, exercise is important. Once you begin a regular exercise program, you'll discover that the benefits to you are not only physical but also psychological. Regular exercise allows you to build your muscles while you're clearing your head and lifting your spirits.

God's instructions are clear: He rewards wise behaviors and He punishes misbehavior. A commitment to a sensible exercise program is one way of being wise, and it's also one way of pleasing God every day. In the space below, give yourself a grade on the quantity and quality of your exercise.

_____

_____

_____

_____

## A FRESH OPPORTUNITY

*Therefore we were buried with Him by baptism into death, in order that, just as Christ was raised from the dead by the glory of the Father, so we too may walk in a new way of life.*

Romans 6:4 HCSB

God's Word is clear: When we genuinely invite Him to reign over our hearts, and when we accept His transforming love, we are forever changed. When we welcome Christ into our hearts, an old life ends and a new way of living—along with a completely new way of viewing the world—begins. Each morning offers a fresh opportunity to invite Christ, yet once again, to rule over our hearts and our days. Each morning presents yet another opportunity to take up His cross and follow in His footsteps. Today, let us rejoice in the new life that is ours through Christ, and let us follow Him, step by step, on the path that He first walked.

In the space below, write down your thoughts about the rewards of letting Christ rule over your heart and your life.

_____

_____

_____

_____

_____

## HOPE FOR THE JOURNEY

*Therefore, we may boldly say: The Lord is my helper; I will not be afraid. What can man do to me?*

Hebrews 13:6 HCSB

Because we are saved by a risen Christ, we can have hope for the future, no matter how desperate our circumstances may seem. After all, God has promised that we are His throughout eternity. And, He has told us that we must place our hopes in Him. Today, summon the courage to follow God. Even if the path seems difficult, even if your heart is fearful, trust your Heavenly Father and follow Him. Trust Him with your day and your life. Do His work, care for His children, and share His Good News. Let Him guide your steps. He will not lead you astray.

In the space below, write down a few of your thoughts about the rewards of following Christ.

## A PRESCRIPTION FOR PANIC

*Anxiety in the heart of man causes depression, but a good word makes it glad.*

Proverbs 12:25 NKJV

We are members of an anxious society, a society in which the changes we face threaten to outpace our abilities to make adjustments. When we're spiritually depleted, the best prescription is found not in the medicine cabinet but deep inside the human heart. What we need is a higher daily dose of God's love, God's peace, God's assurance, and God's presence. And how do we acquire these blessings from our Creator? Through prayer, through meditation, through worship, and through trust.

In the space below, write down your thoughts about God's love for you and your family.

_____

_____

_____

_____

_____

_____

_____

## OUR ULTIMATE SAVIOR

*And we have seen and testify that the Father has sent the Son as Savior of the world.*

1 John 4:14 NKJV

Hannah Whitall Smith spoke to believers of every generation when she advised, "Keep your face upturned to Christ as the flowers do to the sun. Look, and your soul shall live and grow." How true. When we turn our hearts to Jesus, we receive His blessings, His peace, and His grace. Christ is the ultimate Savior of mankind and the personal Savior of those who believe in Him. As His servants, we should place Him at the very center of our lives. And, every day that God gives us breath, we should share Christ's love and His message with a world that needs both.

In the space below, write down your thoughts about Christ's love for you.

_____

_____

_____

_____

_____

_____

## SAYING YES TO GOD

*Fear thou not; for I am with thee.*

Isaiah 41:10 KJV

Your decision to seek a deeper relationship with God will not remove all problems from your life; to the contrary, it will bring about a series of personal crises as you constantly seek to say "yes" to God although the world encourages you to do otherwise. Each time you are tempted to distance yourself from the Creator, you will face a spiritual crisis. A few of these crises may be monumental in scope, but most will be the small, everyday decisions of life. Today, you will face many opportunities to say "yes" to your Creator—and you will also encounter many opportunities to say "no" to Him. Your answers will determine the quality of your day and the direction of your life.

In the space below, write down at least one thing you can do today to say "yes" to God.

_____

_____

_____

_____

_____

_____

## PRACTICING WHAT WE PREACH

*If the way you live isn't consistent with what you believe, then it's wrong.*

Romans 14:23 MSG

In describing our beliefs, our actions are far better descriptors than our words. Yet far too many of us spend more energy talking about our beliefs than living by them—with predictably poor results. As believers, we must beware: Our actions should always give credence to the changes that Christ can make in the lives of those who walk with Him. Is your life a clearly-crafted picture book of your creed? Are your actions always consistent with your beliefs? Are you willing to practice the philosophies that you preach? Hopefully so; otherwise, you'll be tormented by inconsistencies between your beliefs and your behaviors.

In the space below, write down a few thoughts about the rewards that are yours when you live in accordance with your beliefs.

_____

_____

_____

_____

_____

# SPIRITUAL HEALTH,
# SPIRITUAL GROWTH

*But the fruit of the Spirit is love, joy, peace, long-suffering, gentleness, goodness, faith, meekness, temperance . . . .*

Galatians 5:22-23 KJV

Are you as "spiritually fit" as you're ever going to be? Hopefully not! When it comes to your faith (and, by the way, when it comes to your fitness), God isn't done with you yet.

The journey toward spiritual maturity lasts a lifetime: As Christians, we can and should continue to grow in the love and the knowledge of our Savior as long as we live.

Wherever you are in your spiritual journey, it's always the right time to take another step toward God. In the space below, write down something you can do today to take another step with God.

_____

_____

_____

_____

_____

_____

_____

## MEASURING YOUR WORDS

*A wise heart instructs its mouth and increases learning with its speech.*

Proverbs 16:23 HCSB

---

If you seek to be a source of encouragement to friends, to family members, and to coworkers, then you must measure your words carefully. Today, make this promise to yourself: vow to be an honest, effective, encouraging communicator at work, at home, and everyplace in between. Speak wisely, not impulsively. Use words of kindness and praise, not words of anger or derision. Learn how to be truthful without being cruel. Remember that you have the power to heal others or to injure them, to lift others up or to hold them back. And when you learn how to lift them up, you'll soon discover that you've lifted yourself up, too.

---

In the space below, write down at least one thing you can do to improve your skills as a communicator.

---

---

---

---

---

## THE DIRECTION OF YOUR THOUGHTS

*My cup runs over. Surely goodness and mercy shall follow me
all the days of my life; and I will dwell in the house of the Lord
Forever.*

Psalm 23:5-6 NKJV

God has given you free will, including the ability to in-
fluence the direction and the tone of your thoughts. The
quality of your attitude will help determine the quality of
your life, so you must guard your thoughts accordingly.
The next time you find yourself dwelling upon the negative aspects of your life, refocus your attention on things
positive. That's the wise way to direct your thoughts.

If you're a Christian, you have every reason on earth—
and in heaven—to have a positive attitude. In the space
below, offer God thanks for His Word, for His Son, and for
the gift of eternal life.

## IN SEARCH OF WISDOM

*Now if any of you lacks wisdom, he should ask God, who gives to all generously and without criticizing, and it will be given to him. But let him ask in faith without doubting. For the doubter is like the surging sea, driven and tossed by the wind.*

James 1:5-6 HCSB

Where will you find wisdom today? Will you seek it from God or from the world? As a thoughtful Christian living in a society that is filled with temptations and distractions, you know that the world's brand of "wisdom" is everywhere . . . and it is dangerous. Today and every day, as a way of understanding God's plan for your life, you should study His Word and live by it. When you do, you will accumulate a storehouse of wisdom that will enrich your own life and the lives of your family members, your friends, and the world.

God makes His wisdom available to you. In the space below, write down a single Bible verse that you will focus on today.

_____

_____

_____

_____

_____

## SMALL STEPS

*So we must not get tired of doing good, for we will reap at the proper time if we don't give up.*

Galatians 6:9 HCSB

---

If you want to become more physically fit, you don't have to make one giant leap. You can start with many small steps, and you should. When it comes to any new exercise regimen, starting slowly and improving gradually is the smart way to do it.

So if you're determined to improve the state of your health, remember that consistency is the key. Start slowly, avoid injury, be consistent, and expect gradual improvement, not instant success.

---

An exercise program that starts slowly and builds over time is far better than an exercise program that starts—and ends—quickly. In the space below, write down your thoughts on the rewards of perseverance.

_____

_____

_____

_____

_____

_____

## FEEDING THE CHURCH

*The church, you see, is not peripheral to the world; the world is peripheral to the church. The church is Christ's body, in which he speaks and acts, by which he fills everything with his presence.*

Ephesians 1:23 MSG

In the Book of Acts, Luke reminds us to "feed the church of God" (20:28). As Christians who have been saved by a loving, compassionate Creator, we are compelled not only to worship Him in our hearts but also to worship Him in the presence of fellow believers. Do you feed the church of God? Do you attend regularly, and are you an active participant? The answer to these questions will have a profound impact on the quality and direction of your spiritual journey.

In the space below, write down your thoughts about feeding God's church.

_____

_____

_____

_____

_____

_____

## ENOUGH HOURS IN THE DAY?

*It is good to give thanks to the Lord, to sing praises to the Most High. It is good to proclaim your unfailing love in the morning, your faithfulness in the evening.*

Psalm 92:1-2 NLT

Each day has 1,440 minutes—do you value your relationship with God enough to spend a few of those minutes with Him? He deserves that much of your time and more—is He receiving it from you? Hopefully so. But if you find that you're simply "too busy" for a daily chat with your Father in heaven, it's time to take a long, hard look at your priorities and your values. As you consider your plans for the day ahead, here's a tip: organize your life around this simple principle: "God first." When you place your Creator where He belongs—at the very center of your day and your life—the rest of your priorities will fall into place.

In the space below, write down your thoughts about the rewards of studying God's Word.

_____

_____

_____

_____

_____

## LETTING GOD DECIDE

*We can make our plans, but the LORD determines our steps.*

Proverbs 16:9 NLT

Are you facing a difficult decision, a troubling circumstance, or a powerful temptation? If so, it's time to step back, to stop focusing on the world, and to focus, instead, on the will of your Father in heaven. The world will often lead you astray, but God will not. When in doubt, make choices that you sincerely believe will bring you to a closer relationship with God. And if you're uncertain of your next step, pray about it. When you do, answers will come—the right answers for you.

When you've got a choice to make, pray about it—one way to make sure that your heart is in tune with God is to pray often. The more you talk to God, the more He will talk to you. In the space below, write down some decisions you need to pray about.

_____

_____

_____

_____

_____

_____

## MOVING ON

*Do not judge, and you will not be judged. Do not condemn, and you will not be condemned. Forgive, and you will be forgiven.*

Luke 6:37 HCSB

Sometimes, people can be discourteous and cruel. Sometimes people can be unfair, unkind, and unappreciative. So what's a Christian to do? God's answer is straightforward: forgive, forget, and move on. Today and every day, make sure that you're quick to forgive others for their shortcomings. And when other people misbehave (as they most certainly will from time to time), just forgive them as quickly as you can, and try to move on . . . as quickly as you can.

In the space below, write down your thoughts about dealing with difficult people.

_____

_____

_____

_____

_____

_____

_____

## PLANS: YOURS AND GOD'S

*People may make plans in their minds, but the Lord decides what they will do.*

Proverbs 16:9 NCV

If you're like most people, you want things to happen according to your wishes and according to your timetable. But sometimes, God has other plans . . . and He always has the final word.

Are you embittered by a personal tragedy that you did not deserve and cannot understand? If so, it's time to make peace with life. It's time to forgive others, and, if necessary, to forgive yourself. It's time to accept the unchangeable past, to embrace the priceless present, and to have faith in the promise of tomorrow. It's time to trust God completely.

Acceptance means learning to trust God more. Today, write down at least one aspect of your life that you've been reluctant to accept, and then prayerfully ask God to help you trust Him more by accepting the past.

## PROMISES YOU CAN COUNT ON

*God blesses the people who patiently endure testing. Afterward they will receive the crown of life that God has promised to those who love him.*

James 1:12 NLT

Life is often challenging, but as Christians, we must trust the promises of our Heavenly Father. God loves us, and He will protect us. In times of hardship, He will comfort us; in times of sorrow, He will dry our tears. When we are troubled, or weak, or sorrowful, God is with us. His love endures, not only for today, but also for all of eternity.

In the space below, write down your thoughts about the promises that God has made to you.

_____

_____

_____

_____

_____

_____

_____

_____

## GOD CAN HANDLE IT

*Fear not, for I have redeemed you; I have called you by your name; You are Mine.*

Isaiah 43:1 NKJV

---

Life can be difficult and discouraging at times. During our darkest moments, God offers us strength and courage if we turn our hearts and our prayers to Him. The next time you find your courage tested to the limit, remember that God is as near as your next breath. He is your shield and your strength; He is your protector and your deliverer. Call upon Him in your hour of need and then be comforted. Whatever your challenge, whatever your trouble, God can handle it . . . and will!

---

In the space below, write down your thoughts about God's faithfulness and His ability to protect you and your family.

_____

_____

_____

_____

_____

_____

# THE JOURNEY TO IMPROVED FITNESS

*And I pray this: that your love will keep on growing in knowledge and every kind of discernment, so that you can determine what really matters and can be pure and blameless in the day of Christ.*

Philippians 1:9 HCSB

The journey toward improved health is not only a common-sense exercise in personal discipline, it is also a spiritual journey ordained by our Creator. God does not intend that we abuse our bodies by giving in to excessive appetites or to slothful behavior. To the contrary, God has instructed us to protect our physical bodies to the greatest extent we can. In a world that is chock-full of tasty temptations, you may find it all too easy to make unhealthy choices. Your challenge, of course, is to resist those unhealthy choices by every means you can, including prayer.

In the space below, write down several important health issues you need to pray about.

_____

_____

_____

_____

_____

## PRAY CONSTANTLY

*Rejoice in hope; be patient in affliction; be persistent in prayer.*

Romans 12:12 HCSB

God's Word promises that prayer is a powerful tool for changing your life and your world. So here's a question: Are you using prayer as a powerful tool to improve your world, or are you praying sporadically at best? If you're wise, you've learned that prayer is indeed powerful and that it is most powerful when it is used often.

Today, if you haven't already done so, establish the habit of praying constantly. Don't pray day-to-day; pray hour-to-hour. Start each day with prayer, end it with prayer, and fill it with prayer. That's the best way to know God; it's the best way to change your world; and it is, quite simply, the best way to live.

Pray about some of the most important choices that are facing you today.

_____

_____

_____

_____

_____

_____

## TRUSTING GOD'S WILL

*God is my shield, saving those whose hearts are true and right.*

Psalm 7:10 NLT

We face thousands of small choices that make up the fabric of daily life. When we align those choices with God's commandments, and when we align our lives with God's will, we receive His abundance, His peace, and His joy.

Today, you'll face thousands of small choices; as you do, use God's Word as your guide. And, as you face the ultimate choice, place God's Son, God's will, and God's love at the center of your life. You'll discover that God's plan is far grander than any you could have imagined.

Exercising discipline should never be viewed as an imposition or as a form of punishment; far from it. Discipline is the means by which you can take control of your life (which, by the way, is far better than letting your life control you). In the space below, write down your thoughts about the rewards of discipline.

_____

_____

_____

_____

_____

## THE FUTILITY OF BLAME

*Walking down the street, Jesus saw a man blind from birth. His disciples asked, "Rabbi, who sinned: this man or his parents, causing him to be born blind?" Jesus said, "You're asking the wrong question. You're looking for someone to blame. There is no such cause-effect here. Look instead for what God can do."*

John 9:1-3 MSG

To blame others for our own problems is the height of futility. Yet blaming others is a favorite human pastime. Why? Because blaming is much easier than fixing, and criticizing others is so much easier than improving ourselves. Today, instead of looking for someone to blame, look for something to fix, and then get busy fixing it. And as you consider your own situation, remember this: God has a way of helping those who help themselves, but He doesn't spend much time helping those who don't.

In the space below, write down your thoughts about the futility of blame.

_____

_____

_____

_____

_____

_____

## YOU DON'T HAVE TO BE PERFECT

*To acquire wisdom is to love oneself; people who cherish understanding will prosper.*

Proverbs 19:8 NLT

You don't have to be perfect to be wonderful. The difference between perfectionism and realistic expectations is the difference between a life of frustration and a life of contentment. Only one earthly being ever lived life to perfection, and He was the Son of God. The rest of us have fallen short of God's standard and need to be accepting of our own limitations as well as the limitations of others. So, if you've become discouraged with your inability to be perfectly fit, remember that when you accepted Christ as your Savior, God accepted you for all eternity. Now, it's your turn to accept yourself. When you do, you'll feel a tremendous weight being lifted from your shoulders.

In the space below, write down your thoughts about what it really means to please God.

_____

_____

_____

_____

_____

_____

## THE POWER OF PERSEVERANCE

*I do not consider myself to have taken hold of it. But one thing I do: forgetting what is behind and reaching forward to what is ahead, I pursue as my goal the prize promised by God's heavenly call in Christ Jesus.*

Philippians 3:13-14 HCSB

It's simply a fact of life: Not all of your health-related plans will succeed, and not all of your goals will be met. Hebrews 10:36 advises, "Patient endurance is what you need now, so you will continue to do God's will. Then you will receive all that he has promised" (NLT). These words remind us that when we persevere, we will eventually receive the rewards which God has promised us. What's required is perseverance, not perfection.

In the space below, write down your thoughts about the power of perseverance.

_____

_____

_____

_____

_____

_____

## THE PURSUIT OF GOD'S TRUTH

*But grow in the grace and knowledge of our Lord and Savior Jesus Christ. To Him be the glory both now and forever. Amen.*

2 Peter 3:18 NKJV

Have you established a passionate relationship with God's Holy Word? Hopefully so. After all, the Bible is a roadmap for life here on earth and for life eternal. The words of Matthew 4:4 remind us that, "Man shall not live by bread alone but by every word that proceedeth out of the mouth of God" (KJV). As believers, we must study the Bible and meditate upon its meaning for our lives. Otherwise, we deprive ourselves of a priceless gift from our Creator. God's Holy Word is, indeed, a transforming gift from the Father in heaven.

In the space below, write down your thoughts about the importance of Bible study.

_____

_____

_____

_____

_____

_____

_____

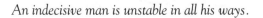

## DECISION-MAKING 101

*An indecisive man is unstable in all his ways.*

James 1:8 HCSB

---

If you're facing one of life's major decisions, here are some things you can do: 1. Gather as much information as you can. 2. Don't be too impulsive. 3. Rely on the advice of trusted friends and mentors. 4. Pray for guidance. 5. Trust the quiet inner voice of your conscience. 6. When the time for action arrives, act. Procrastination is the enemy of progress; don't let it defeat you. People who can never quite seem to make up their minds usually make themselves miserable. So when in doubt, be decisive. It's the decent way to live.

---

In the space below, write down an important task that you've been putting off. Then, pray for God's guidance and trust the guidance He gives.

---

---

---

---

---

---

## WHAT DOESN'T CHANGE

*Jesus Christ is the same yesterday, today, and forever.*

Hebrews 13:8 HCSB

Our world is in a state of constant change. God is not. At times, the world seems to be trembling beneath our feet. But we can be comforted in the knowledge that our Heavenly Father is the rock that cannot be shaken. His Word promises, "I am the Lord, I do not change" (Malachi 3:6 NKJV). Every day that we live, we mortals encounter a multitude of changes—some good, some not so good, some downright disheartening. On those occasions when we must endure life-changing personal losses that leave us breathless, there is a place we can turn for comfort and assurance—we can turn to God. He is unchanging, and His love endures forever.

In the space below, write down your thoughts about some of the changes that are currently taking place in your life.

_____

_____

_____

_____

_____

_____

## COUNTING YOUR BLESSINGS

*Finally, brethren, whatever things are true, whatever things are noble, whatever things are just, whatever things are pure, whatever things are lovely, whatever things are of good report, if there is any virtue and if there is anything praiseworthy— meditate on these things.*

Philippians 4:8 NKJV

How will you direct your thoughts today? Will you obey the words of Philippians 4:8 by dwelling upon those things that are noble, true, and lovely? Or will you allow your thoughts to be hijacked by the negativity that seems to dominate our troubled world? God intends that you experience joy and abundance. So, today and every day hereafter, celebrate the life that God has given you by focusing your thoughts upon those things that are worthy of praise.

In the space below, jot down a few of your thoughts about the advantages of maintaining a positive attitude.

_____

_____

_____

_____

_____

_____

## NEED SOMETHING FROM GOD? ASK!

*You do not have because you do not ask.*

James 4:2 HCSB

James 5:16 makes a promise that God intends to keep: when you pray earnestly, fervently, and often, great things will happen. Too many people, however, are too timid or too pessimistic to ask God to do big things. Please don't count yourself among their number. God can do great things through you if you have the courage to ask Him (and the determination to keep asking Him). But don't expect Him to do all the work. When you do your part, He will do His part—and when He does, you can expect miracles to happen.

Today, write down a specific need that is weighing heavily on your heart. Then, spend a few quiet moments asking God for His guidance and for His help.

_____

_____

_____

_____

_____

_____

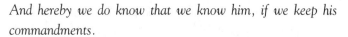

## OBEDIENCE NOW

*And hereby we do know that we know him, if we keep his commandments.*

1 John 2:3 KJV

---

In order to enjoy a deeper relationship with God, you must strive diligently to live in accordance with His commandments. But there's a problem—you live in a world that seeks to snare your attention and lead you away from God. You cannot be perfectly obedient, nor does God expect you to be. What is required is a sincere desire to be obedient coupled with an awareness of sin and a willingness to distance yourself from it as soon as you encounter it. Are you willing to conform your behavior to God's rules? Hopefully, you can answer that question with a yes. Otherwise, you'll never experience a full measure of the blessings that the Creator gives to those who obey Him.

---

In the space below, write down a few thoughts about the rewards of being an obedient Christian.

---

---

---

---

---

## KEEPING UP APPEARANCES

*For am I now trying to win the favor of people, or God? Or am I striving to please people? If I were still trying to please people, I would not be a slave of Christ.*

Galatians 1:10 HCSB

Are you worried about keeping up appearances? And as a result, do you spend too much time, energy, or money on things that are intended to make you look good? If so, you are certainly not alone. Ours is a society that focuses intently upon appearances. We are told time and again that we can't be "too thin or too rich." But in truth, the important things in life have little to do with food, fashion, fame, or fortune. Today, focus on pleasing God and don't worry too much about trying to impress the folks you happen to pass on the street.

In the space below, write down a few thoughts about the difference between pleasing God and pleasing people.

_____

_____

_____

_____

_____

_____

## HIS INFINITE LOVE

*For I am persuaded that neither death nor life, nor angels nor rulers, nor things present, nor things to come, nor powers, nor height, nor depth, nor any other created thing will have the power to separate us from the love of God that is in Christ Jesus our Lord!*

Romans 8:38-39 HCSB

Christ's love for you is personal. He loves you so much that He gave His life in order that you might spend all eternity with Him. Christ loves you individually and intimately; His is a love unbounded by time or circumstance. Are you willing to experience an intimate relationship with Him? Your Savior is waiting patiently; don't make Him wait a single minute longer. Embrace His love today.

In the space below, write down a few of your thoughts about Christ's love for you.

_____

_____

_____

_____

_____

_____

_____

## BEYOND ANXIETY

*In the multitude of my anxieties within me, Your comforts delight my soul.*

Psalm 94:19 NKJV

---

God calls us to live above and beyond anxiety. God calls us to live by faith, not by fear. He instructs us to trust Him completely, this day and forever. But sometimes, trusting God is difficult, especially when we become caught up in the incessant demands of an anxious world. When you feel anxious—and you will—return your thoughts to God's love. Then, take your concerns to Him in prayer, and to the best of your ability, leave them there. Whatever "it" is, God is big enough to handle it. Let Him. Now.

---

Remembering God's faithfulness in the past can give you peace for today and hope for tomorrow. In the space below, write down your thoughts about God's faithfulness.

_____

_____

_____

_____

_____

_____

_____

## SOLVING LIFE'S RIDDLES

*If you need wisdom—if you want to know what God wants you to do—ask him, and he will gladly tell you. He will not resent your asking.*

James 1:5 NLT

Life presents each of us with countless questions, conundrums, doubts, and problems. Thankfully, the riddles of everyday living are not too difficult to solve if we look for answers in the right places. When we have questions, we should consult God's Word, we should seek the guidance of the Holy Spirit, and we should trust the counsel of God-fearing friends and family members. Are you facing a difficult decision? Take your concerns to God. When you do, He will speak to you in His own way and in His own time, and when He does, you can most certainly trust the answers that He gives.

In the space below, write down your thoughts about an important decision you need to start praying about.

_____

_____

_____

_____

_____

_____

## NOW, NOT LATER

*We can't afford to waste a minute, must not squander these precious daylight hours in frivolity and indulgence . . . . Don't loiter and linger, waiting until the very last minute. Dress yourselves in Christ, and be up and about!*

Romans 13:13-14 MSG

Procrastination results from an individual's short-sighted attempt to postpone temporary discomfort. Once you acquire the habit of doing what needs to be done when it needs to be done, you will avoid untold trouble, worry, and stress. So learn to defeat procrastination by paying less attention to your fears and more attention to your responsibilities. God has created a world that punishes procrastinators and rewards women who "do it now." Life doesn't procrastinate—neither should you.

In the space below, write down an important obligation that you've been putting off. Then, pray for God's strength and His guidance.

_____

_____

_____

_____

_____

_____

## PERFECTION ISN'T REQUIRED

*If you wait for perfect conditions, you will never get anything done.*

Ecclesiastes 11:4 NLT

---

As you begin to work toward improved physical and emotional health, don't expect perfection. Of course you should work hard; of course you should be disciplined; of course you should do your best. But then, when you've given it your best effort, you should be accepting of yourself, imperfect though you may be. In heaven, we will know perfection. Here on earth, we have a few short years to wrestle with the challenges of imperfection. Let us accept these lives that God has given us—and these bodies which are ours for a brief time here on earth—with open, loving arms.

---

In the space below, write down your thoughts on the dangers of perfectionism.

_____

_____

_____

_____

_____

_____

## FACING UP TO TROUBLE

*I will be with you when you pass through the waters . . . when you walk through the fire . . . the flame will not burn you. For I the Lord your God, the Holy One of Israel, and your Savior.*

Isaiah 43:2-3 HCSB

As life-here-on-earth unfolds, all of us encounter occasional setbacks: Those occasional visits from Old Man Trouble are simply a fact of life, and none of us are exempt. When tough times arrive, we may be forced to rearrange our plans and our priorities. But even on our darkest days, we must remember that God's love remains constant. The fact that we encounter adversity is not nearly so important as the way we choose to deal with it.

In the space below, write down your thoughts about the best ways to deal with tough times.

_____

_____

_____

_____

_____

_____

_____

_____

# YOUR FITNESS IS YOUR RESPONSIBILITY

*Each will receive his own reward according to his own labor. Each man's work will become evident.*

1 Corinthians 3:8,13 NASB

Do you sincerely desire to improve your physical fitness? If so, start by taking personal responsibility for the body that God has given you. Then, make the solemn pledge to yourself that you will begin to make the changes that are required to enjoy a longer, healthier, happier life.

Today, write down one or two small steps you can take to improve your physical and spiritual health.

_____

_____

_____

_____

_____

_____

_____

_____

_____

## A GROWING RELATIONSHIP WITH GOD

*But grow in the grace and knowledge of our Lord and Savior Jesus Christ. To Him be the glory both now and to the day of eternity.*

2 Peter 3:18 HCSB

As each new day unfolds, you are confronted with a wide range of decisions: how you will behave, where you will direct your thoughts, with whom you will associate, and what you will choose to worship. These choices, along with many others like them, are yours and yours alone. How you choose determines how your relationship with God will unfold.

Are you continuing to grow in your love and knowledge of the Lord? Hopefully, you're determined to make yourself a growing Christian. Your Savior deserves no less, and neither, by the way, do you. In the space below, write down your thoughts about your relationship with Jesus.

_____

_____

_____

_____

_____

# HUMBLED BY HIS SACRIFICE

*But as for me, I will never boast about anything except the cross of our Lord Jesus Christ, through whom the world has been crucified to me, and I to the world.*

Galatians 6:14 HCSB

As we consider Christ's sacrifice on the cross, we should be profoundly humbled. And today, as we come to Christ in prayer, we should do so in a spirit of humble devotion.

Christ humbled Himself on a cross—for you. He shed His blood—for you. He has offered to walk with you through this life and throughout all eternity. As you approach Him today in prayer, think about His sacrifice and His grace. And be humble.

In the space below, write down a few of your thoughts about Christ's sacrifice.

_____

_____

_____

_____

_____

_____

_____

## CELEBRATION!

*Celebrate God all day, every day. I mean, revel in him!*

Philippians 4:4 MSG

---

This day is presented to us fresh and clean at midnight, free of charge, but we must beware: Today is a non-renewable resource—once it's gone, it's gone forever. Our responsibility, of course, is to use this day in the service of God's will and according to His commandments. Today, treasure the time that God has given you. Give Him the glory and the praise and the thanksgiving that He deserves. And search for the hidden possibilities that God has placed along your path. This day is a priceless gift from God, so use it joyfully and encourage others to do likewise. After all, this is the day the Lord has made....

---

God has given you the gift of life and the promise of eternal life. In the space below, write down a few of your thoughts about God's love for you.

_____

_____

_____

_____

_____

_____

## IT PAYS TO STAY RESTED

*I find rest in God; only he gives me hope.*

Psalm 62:5 NCV

You live in a world that tempts you to stay up late—very late. But too much late-night TV, combined with too little sleep, is a prescription for exhaustion, ill health, ill temper, or all three. So do yourself and your loved ones a big favor. Arrange your TV schedule and your life so you get eight hours of sleep every night. Since you can't cheat Mr. Sandman, don't even try. When in doubt, do the smart thing: do whatever it takes to get the sleep you need. It's the smart way to schedule your day and your life.

In the space below, write down one or two specific things you can do to improve the quantity or quality of your sleep.

_____

_____

_____

_____

_____

_____

_____

## TOO FRIENDLY WITH THE WORLD?

*Let no one deceive himself. If anyone among you seems to be wise in this age, let him become a fool that he may become wise. For the wisdom of this world is foolishness with God. For it is written, "He catches the wise in their own craftiness."*

1 Corinthians 3:18–19 NKJV

The world in which we live is a noisy, distracting place, a place that seems to cry, "Worship me with your time, your money, your energy, your thoughts, and your life!" But if we are wise, we won't fall prey to that temptation. If you desire a healthier lifestyle, you must distance yourself from the temptations and distractions of modern-day society.

The world makes plenty of promises that it can't keep. God, on the other hand, keeps every single one of His promises. Jot down some areas of your life that you need to turn over to God.

_____

_____

_____

_____

_____

_____

_____

## CHEERFUL CHRISTIANITY

*Be cheerful. Keep things in good repair. Keep your spirits up.
Think in harmony. Be agreeable. Do all that, and the God of
love and peace will be with you for sure.*

2 Corinthians 13:11 MSG

Mrs. Charles E. Cowman wrote, "Two wings are necessary
to lift our souls toward God: prayer and praise. Prayer asks.
Praise accepts the answer." That's why we should find the
time to lift our concerns to God in prayer, and to praise
Him for all that He has done. Our challenge, of course, is
to ensure that Satan cannot use these tools on us.

Are you a cheerful Christian? You should be! And
what is the best way to attain the joy that is rightfully
yours? By giving Christ what is rightfully His: your heart,
your soul, and your life.

In the space below, write down your thoughts about the
rewards of being a cheerful Christian.

_____

_____

_____

_____

_____

_____

## FACING LIFE'S TRIALS

*So because of Christ, I am pleased in weaknesses, in insults, in catastrophes, in persecutions, and in pressures. For when I am weak, then I am strong.*

2 Corinthians 12:10 HCSB

Life is a tapestry of good days and difficult days, with good days predominating. During the good days, we are tempted to take our blessings for granted (a temptation that we must resist with all our might). But, during life's difficult days, we discover precisely what we're made of. And more importantly, we discover what our faith is made of. When your faith is put to the test, rest assured that God is perfectly willing—and always ready—to give you strength for the struggle.

In the space below, write down your thoughts about God's faithfulness.

_____

_____

_____

_____

_____

_____

_____

## GOD IS HERE

*Draw near to God, and He will draw near to you.*

James 4:8 HCSB

God is constantly making Himself available to you; therefore, when you approach Him obediently and sincerely, You will most certainly find Him: God is always available to you. Whenever it seems to you that God is distant, disinterested, or altogether absent, you may rest assured that your feelings are a reflection of your own emotional state, not an indication of God's absence. If, during life's darker days, you seek to establish a closer relationship with Him, you can do so because God is not just near, He is here.

In the space below, write down your thoughts about the rewards of growing near to God.

_____

_____

_____

_____

_____

_____

_____

## HE WILL GIVE YOU STRENGTH

*Those who hope in the LORD will renew their strength. They will soar on wings like eagles; they will run and not grow weary, they will walk and not be faint*

Isaiah 40:31 NIV

As you make the journey toward improved fitness, you'll undoubtedly run out of energy from time to time. When it happens, you can turn to God for strength and for guidance.

Andrew Murray observed, "Where there is much prayer, there will be much of the Spirit; where there is much of the Spirit, there will be ever-increasing power." These words remind us that the ultimate source of our strength is God. Are you feeling exhausted? Are your emotions on edge? If so, it's time to turn things over to God in prayer.

For the journey through life, you need energy. The best source of energy, of course, is God. In the space below, write down your thoughts about God's strength.

## NOURISHED BY THE WORD

*You will be a good servant of Christ Jesus, nourished by the words of the faith and of the good teaching that you have followed.*

1 Timothy 4:6 HCSB

As you establish priorities for life, you must decide if God's Word will be a bright spotlight that guides your path every day or a tiny nightlight that occasionally flickers in the dark. The decision to study the Bible is yours and yours alone. But make no mistake: how you choose to use your Bible will have a profound impact on you and your loved ones. The Bible is the ultimate guide for life; make it your guidebook as well.

In the space below, write down your thoughts about the role that God's Word should play in the life of your family.

_____

_____

_____

_____

_____

_____

_____

## A RELATIONSHIP THAT HONORS GOD

*I am always praising you; all day long I honor you.*

Psalm 71:8 NCV

As you think about the nature of your relationship with God, remember this: you will always have some type of relationship with Him—it is inevitable that your life must be lived in relationship to God. Are you willing to place God first in your life? And, are you willing to welcome God's Son into your heart? Unless you can honestly answer these questions with a resounding yes, then your relationship with God isn't what it could be or should be. Thankfully, God is always available, He's always ready to forgive, and He's waiting to hear from you now. The rest, of course, is up to you.

In the space below, write down your thoughts about the wisdom of putting God first in your life.

_____

_____

_____

_____

_____

_____

# THE NEED TO BE DISCIPLINED

*Do you not know that the runners in a stadium all race, but only one receives the prize? Run in such a way that you may win. Now everyone who competes exercises self-control in everything. However, they do it to receive a perishable crown, but we an imperishable one.*

1 Corinthians 9:24-25 HCSB

God is clear: we must exercise self-discipline in all matters. Self-discipline is not simply a proven way to get ahead, it's also an integral part of God's plan for our lives. If we genuinely seek to be faithful stewards of our time, our talents, and our resources, we must adopt a disciplined approach to life. Otherwise, our talents are wasted and our resources are squandered. Our greatest rewards result from hard work and perseverance. May we, as disciplined believers, be willing to work for the rewards we so earnestly desire.

When it comes to your health, it's always the right time to start establishing the right habits. In the space below, write down a change that you need to make today.

_____

_____

_____

_____

_____

## NOW IS THE TIME

*So, my son, throw yourself into this work for Christ.*

2 Timothy 1:1 MSG

God's love for you is deeper and more profound than you can imagine. God's love for you is so great that He sent His only Son to this earth to die for your sins and to offer you the priceless gift of eternal life. Now, you must decide whether or not to accept God's gift. Your decision to allow Christ to reign over your heart is the pivotal decision of your life. It is a decision that you cannot ignore. It is a decision that is yours and yours alone. Accept God's gift now: allow His Son to preside over your heart, your thoughts, and your life, starting this very instant.

In the space below, write down your thoughts about following Christ.

_____

_____

_____

_____

_____

_____

_____

## LEARNING WHEN TO SAY NO

*So let us run the race that is before us and never give up. We should remove from our lives anything that would get in the way and the sin that so easily holds us back.*

Hebrews 12:1 NCV

If you're like most women, you've got plenty of people pulling you in lots of directions. Perhaps you have responsibilities at home, work, church or in any of a hundred other activities that gobble up big portions of your day. If so, you'll need to be sure that you know when to say enough is enough. When it comes to squeezing more and more obligations onto your daily to-do list, you have the right to say no when you simply don't have the time, the energy, or the desire to do the job.

You have a right to say no. Don't feel guilty about asserting that right. In the space below, write down your thoughts about the benefits of being able to say no when necessary.

_____

_____

_____

_____

_____

_____

# DAY 142

## HEARING THE CALL

*One thing I do, forgetting those things which are behind and reaching forward to those things which are ahead, I press toward the goal for the prize of the upward call of God in Christ Jesus.*

Philippians 3:13-14 NKJV

It is vitally important that you heed God's call. In John 15:16, Jesus says, "You did not choose me, but I chose you and appointed you to go and bear fruit—fruit that will last" (NIV). In other words, you have been called by Christ, and now it is up to you to decide precisely how you will answer. Have you already found your special calling? If so, you're a very lucky person. If not, keep searching and keep praying until you discover it. And remember this: God has important work for you to do—work that no one else on earth can accomplish but you.

In the space below, write down your thoughts about the role that God should play in your plans for the future.

_____

_____

_____

_____

_____

## DEALING WITH DISAPPOINTMENT

*For we do not want you to be ignorant, brethren, of our trouble which came to us in Asia: that we were burdened beyond measure, above strength, so that we despaired even of life. Yes, we had the sentence of death in ourselves, that we should not trust in ourselves but in God who raises the dead, who delivered us from so great a death, and does deliver us; in whom we trust that He will still deliver us.*

2 Corinthians 1:8-10 NKJV

From time to time, all of us face life-altering disappointments that leave us breathless. Oftentimes, these disappointments come unexpectedly, leaving us with more questions than answers. But even when we don't have all the answers, God does. Whatever our circumstances, God is ready to protect us, to comfort us, and to heal us.

In the space below, write down your thoughts about dealing with life's inevitable disappointments.

_____

_____

_____

_____

_____

_____

## GROWING IN CHRIST

*When I was a child, I spoke like a child, I thought like a child,
I reasoned like a child. When I became a man, I put aside
childish things.*

1 Corinthians 13:11 HCSB

As Christians, we can and should continue to grow in the
love and the knowledge of our Savior as long as we live.
Norman Vincent Peale had the following advice for believers of all ages: "Ask the God who made you to keep re-
making you." That advice, of course, is perfectly sound, but
often ignored. When we cease to grow, either emotionally
or spiritually, we do ourselves a profound disservice. But, if
we study God's Word, if we obey His commandments, and
if we live in the center of His will, we will not be stagnant
believers; we will, instead, be growing Christians.

In the space below, write down your thoughts about your
own spiritual journey.

_____

_____

_____

_____

_____

_____

# DO IT NOW

*Don't be deceived: God is not mocked. For whatever a man sows he will also reap, because the one who sows to his flesh will reap corruption from the flesh, but the one who sows to the Spirit will reap eternal life from the Spirit.*

Galatians 6:7-8 HCSB

Healthy choices are easy to put off until some future date. But procrastination, especially concerning matters of personal health, is, at best, foolish and, at worst, dangerous. If you feel the need to improve your physical health, don't wait for New Year's Day; don't even wait until tomorrow. The time to begin living a healthier life is the moment you finish reading this sentence.

In the space below, write down your thoughts about an important task you need to begin today.

_____

_____

_____

_____

_____

_____

_____

## PERFECT WISDOM

*Therefore, everyone who hears these words of Mine and acts on them will be like a sensible man who built his house on the rock. The rain fell, the rivers rose, and the winds blew and pounded that house. Yet it didn't collapse, because its foundation was on the rock.*

Matthew 7:24-25 HCSB

Where will you place your trust today? Will you trust in the wisdom of fallible men and women, or will you place your faith in God's perfect wisdom? Where you choose to place your trust will determine the direction and quality of your life.

Are you tired? Discouraged? Fearful? Be comforted and trust God. Are you worried or anxious? Be confident in God's power and trust His Holy Word. He is not a God of confusion. Talk with Him; listen to Him; trust Him. He is steadfast, and He is your protector . . . forever.

In the space below, write down your thoughts about the power of God's Word.

_____

_____

_____

_____

## BEYOND GUILT

*There is therefore now no condemnation to those who are in Christ Jesus, who do not walk according to the flesh, but according to the Spirit.*

Romans 8:1 NKJV

All of us have sinned. Sometimes our sins result from our own stubborn rebellion against God's commandments. And sometimes, we are swept up in events that are beyond our abilities to control. Under either set of circumstances, we may experience intense feelings of guilt. But God has an answer for the guilt that we feel. That answer, of course, is His forgiveness. Are you troubled by feelings of guilt or regret? If so, you must ask your Heavenly Father for His forgiveness. When you do so, He will forgive you completely and without reservation. Then, you must forgive yourself just as God has forgiven you: thoroughly and unconditionally.

In the space below, write down your thoughts about God's forgiveness.

_____

_____

_____

_____

_____

## SEEKING GOD AND
## FINDING HAPPINESS

*Happy is the one whose help is the God of Jacob, whose hope is in the Lord his God.*

Psalm 146:5 HCSB

Happiness depends less upon our circumstances than upon our thoughts. When we turn our thoughts to God, to His gifts, and to His glorious creation, we experience the joy that God intends for His children. But, when we focus on the negative aspects of life, we suffer. Do you sincerely want to be a happy Christian? Then set your mind and your heart upon God's love and His grace. The fullness of life in Christ is available to all who seek it and claim it. Count yourself among that number. Seek first the salvation that is available through a personal relationship with Jesus Christ, and then claim the joy, the peace, and the spiritual abundance that the Shepherd offers His sheep.

In the space below, write down a few of your ideas about happiness.

_____

_____

_____

_____

_____

## WHEN PEOPLE MISBEHAVE

*Bad temper is contagious—don't get infected.*

Proverbs 22:25 MSG

Face it: sometimes people can be rude . . . very rude. When other people are unkind to you, you may be tempted to strike back, either verbally or in some other way. Don't do it! Instead, remember that God corrects other people's behaviors in His own way, and He doesn't need your help (even if you're totally convinced that He does). So, when other people behave cruelly, foolishly, or impulsively—as they will from time to time—don't be hotheaded. Instead, speak up for yourself as politely as you can, and walk away. Then, forgive everybody as quickly as you can, and leave the rest up to God.

In the space below, write down your thoughts about dealing with difficult people.

_____

_____

_____

_____

_____

_____

_____

## GETTING IT ALL DONE

*Everyone was trying to touch him—so much energy surging from him, so many people healed!*

Luke 6:19 MSG

All of us suffer through difficult days, trying times, and perplexing periods of our lives. During times of hardship, we are tempted to burn the candle at both ends, but we should resist this temptation. Instead, we should strive to place first things first by saying no to the things that we simply don't have the time or the energy to do. If you're a person with too many demands and too few hours in which to meet them, don't fret. Instead, ask God for the wisdom to prioritize your life and the strength to fulfill your responsibilities. God will give you the energy to do the most important things on today's to-do list…if you ask Him. So ask Him.

In the space below, write down a few of the benefits that can be yours when you organize and prioritize your to-do list.

_____

_____

_____

_____

_____

# DAY 151

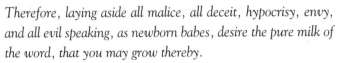

## BEYOND ENVY

*Therefore, laying aside all malice, all deceit, hypocrisy, envy, and all evil speaking, as newborn babes, desire the pure milk of the word, that you may grow thereby.*

1 Peter 2:1-2 NKJV

Because we are frail, imperfect human beings, we are sometimes envious of others. But God's Word warns us that envy is sin. Thus, we must guard ourselves against the natural tendency to feel resentment and jealousy when other people experience good fortune. As believers, we have absolutely no reason to be envious of any people on earth. After all, as Christians we are already recipients of the greatest gift in all creation: God's grace. We have been promised the gift of eternal life through God's only begotten Son, and we must count that gift as our most precious possession.

In the space below, write down your thoughts about the futility of envy.

_____

_____

_____

_____

_____

_____

## YOU'RE ACCOUNTABLE

*But each person should examine his own work, and then he will have a reason for boasting in himself alone, and not in respect to someone else. For each person will have to carry his own load.*

Galatians 6:4-5 HCSB

Whether you like it or not, you (and only you) are accountable for your actions. But because you are human, you'll be sorely tempted to pass the blame. Avoid that temptation at all costs. Problem-solving builds character. Every time you straighten your back and look squarely into the face of Old Man Trouble, you'll strengthen not only your backbone but also your spirit.

It's easy to hold other people accountable, but real accountability begins with the person in the mirror. Think about one specific area of responsibility that is uniquely yours, and then write down one specific step you can take today to better fulfill that responsibility.

_____

_____

_____

_____

_____

_____

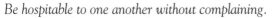

## BEYOND COMPLAINING

*Be hospitable to one another without complaining.*

1 Peter 4:9 HCSB

Most of us have more blessings than we can count, yet we can still find reasons to complain about the minor frustrations of everyday life. To do so, of course, is not only short-sighted, but it is also a serious roadblock on the path to spiritual abundance. Would you like to feel more comfortable about your circumstances and your life? Then promise yourself that you'll do whatever it takes to ensure that you focus your thoughts and energy on the major blessings you've received, not the minor inconveniences you must occasionally endure.

The next time you're tempted to complain about the inevitable frustrations of everyday living, don't do it. Instead, make it a practice to count your blessings, not your hardships. It's the truly healthy way to live. In the space below, write a few of the ways that God has blessed you and your family.

_____

_____

_____

_____

_____

## THE GIFT OF LIFE

*What a gift life is to those who stay the course! You've heard, of course, of Job's staying power, and you know how God brought it all together for him at the end. That's because God cares, cares right down to the last detail.*

James 5:11 MSG

This day, like every other, is filled to the brim with opportunities, challenges, and choices. But, no choice that you make is more important than the choice you make concerning where you place God in your life. Sometimes, we don't intentionally neglect God; we simply allow ourselves to become overwhelmed with the demands of everyday life. And then, without our even realizing it, we gradually drift away from the One we need most. Thankfully, God never drifts away from us. He remains always present, always steadfast, always loving.

Life is a priceless gift from God. Spend time each day thanking God for His gift. Start today in the space below.

_____

_____

_____

_____

_____

## COMPETENCE, YES. EXCUSES, NO!

*Do you see people skilled in their work? They will work for kings, not for ordinary people.*

Proverbs 22:29 NCV

Excuses are everywhere . . . excellence is not. If you seek excellence (and the rewards that accompany it), you must avoid the bad habit of making excuses. Whatever your job description, it's up to you, and no one else, to become a master of your craft. It's up to you to do your job right— and to do it right now. When you do, you'll discover that excellence is its own reward . . . but not its only reward.

In the space below, write down your thoughts about the destructiveness of excuses.

_____

_____

_____

_____

_____

_____

_____

_____

_____

## IN HIS HANDS

*For whatever is born of God overcomes the world. And this is the victory that has overcome the world—our faith.*

1 John 5:4 NKJV

---

The first element of a successful life is faith: faith in God, faith in His Son, and faith in His promises. If we place our lives in God's hands, our faith is rewarded in ways that we—as human beings with clouded vision and limited understanding—can scarcely comprehend. But, if we seek to rely solely upon our own resources, or if we seek earthly success outside the boundaries of God's commandments, we reap a bitter harvest for ourselves and for our loved ones. Do you desire the abundance and success that God has promised? Then trust Him today and every day that you live.

---

In the space below, write down your thoughts about entrusting your future to God.

_____

_____

_____

_____

_____

_____

# GOD REWARDS DISCIPLINE

*The one who follows instruction is on the path to life, but the one who rejects correction goes astray.*

Proverbs 10:17 HCSB

Wise women understand the importance of discipline. In Proverbs 28:19, God's message is clear: "He who works his land will have abundant food, but the one who chases fantasies will have his fill of poverty" (NIV). When we work diligently and consistently, we can expect a bountiful harvest. But we must never expect the harvest to precede the labor. Thoughtful Christians understand that God doesn't reward laziness or misbehavior. To the contrary, God expects His children (of all ages) to lead disciplined lives . . . very disciplined lives.

In the space below, write down your thoughts about the need to be disciplined.

_____

_____

_____

_____

_____

_____

_____

# YOU AND YOUR CONSCIENCE

*Blessed is the man who does not condemn himself.*

Romans 14:22 HCSB

God gave each of us a conscience for a very good reason: to listen to it. Wise believers make it a practice to listen carefully to that quiet internal voice. Count yourself among that number. When your conscience speaks, listen and learn. In all likelihood, God is trying to get His message through. Few things in life torment us more than a guilty conscience. And, few things in life provide more contentment than the knowledge that we are obeying God's commandments and following His will.

If you're genuinely planning on becoming a disciplined person "some day" in the distant future, you're deluding yourself. The best day to begin exercising self-discipline is this one. In the space below, write down your thoughts about the need to focus on important tasks sooner rather than later.

_____

_____

_____

_____

_____

_____

## THE POWER OF PATIENCE

*Be gentle to everyone, able to teach, and patient.*

2 Timothy 2:23 HCSB

---

The best things in life seldom happen overnight; they usually take time. Henry Blackaby writes, "The grass that is here today and gone tomorrow does not require much time to mature. A big oak tree that lasts for generations requires much more time to grow and mature. God is concerned about your life through eternity. Allow Him to take all the time He needs to shape you for His purposes. Larger assignments will require longer periods of preparation." How true.

---

Every step of your life's journey is a choice . . . and the quality of those choices determines the quality of the journey. In the space below, write down at least one wise choice that you need to make today.

## KEEP MAKING PROGRESS

*For a righteous man may fall seven times and rise again.*

Proverbs 24:16 NKJV

Spiritual growth is not instantaneous . . . and neither, for that matter, is the attainment of a physically fit body. So be patient. You should expect a few ups and downs along the way, but you should also expect to see progress over time.

Take a careful look inside your refrigerator. Are the contents reflective of a healthy lifestyle? And if your fridge is overflowing with junk foods, write down all the items that you won't purchase again.

_____

_____

_____

_____

_____

_____

_____

_____

_____

_____

## CONTAGIOUS CHRISTIANITY

*We are therefore Christ's ambassadors, as though God were making his appeal through us. We implore you on Christ's behalf: Be reconciled to God.*

2 Corinthians 5:20 NIV

Genuine, heartfelt Christianity can be highly contagious. When you've experienced the transforming power of God's love, you feel the need to share the Good News of His only begotten Son. So, whether you realize it or not, you can be sure that you are being led to share the story of your faith with family, with friends, and with the world.

Every believer bears responsibility for sharing God's Good News. And it is important to remember that you share your testimony through words and actions. Today, don't be bashful or timid: Talk about Jesus and, while you're at it, show the world what it really means to follow Him.

In the space below, write down your thoughts about your relationship with Jesus.

_____

_____

_____

_____

_____

## DISCOVERING GOD'S POWER

*God is strong, and he wants you strong.*

Ephesians 6:10 MSG

Even the most inspired Christians can, from time to time, find themselves running on empty. The demands of daily life can drain us of our strength and rob us of the joy that is rightfully ours in Christ. When we find ourselves tired, discouraged, or worse, there is a source from which we can draw the power needed to restore our souls. That source of power is God.

In the space below, jot down your thoughts about the energizing power of prayer.

_____

_____

_____

_____

_____

_____

_____

_____

_____

## ACCEPTING GOD'S CALLING

*But as God has distributed to each one, as the Lord has called each one, so let him walk.*

1 Corinthians 7:17 NKJV

God is calling you to follow a specific path that He has chosen for your life. And it is vitally important that you heed that call. Otherwise, your talents and opportunities may go unused. If you have not yet discovered what God intends for you to do with your life, keep searching and keep praying until you discover why the Creator put you here. Remember: God has important work for you to do—work that no one else on earth can accomplish but you. The Creator has placed you in a particular location, amid particular people, with unique opportunities to serve. And He has given you all the tools you need to succeed. So listen for His voice, watch for His signs, and prepare yourself for the call that is sure to come.

In the space below, jot down your thoughts about the importance of heeding God's call.

_____

_____

_____

_____

_____

## WITH GOD'S STRENGTH

*Come to Me, all you who are weary and burdened, and I will give you rest. Take My yoke upon you and learn from Me, because I am gentle and humble in heart, and you will find rest for your souls. For My yoke is easy and My burden is light.*

Matthew 11:28–30 HCSB

---

Are you tired or discouraged? Ask God for strength. Perhaps you are in a hurry for God to reveal His plans for your life. If so, be forewarned: God operates on His own timetable, not yours. Sometimes, God may answer your prayers with silence, and when He does, you must patiently persevere. Whatever your problem, He can handle it. Your job is to keep persevering until He does.

---

Becoming fit—and staying fit—is an exercise in perseverance. If you give up at the first sign of trouble, you won't accomplish much. But if you don't give up, you'll eventually improve your health and your life. In the space below, write down a few of your thoughts about the need to persevere.

---

---

---

---

---

## SEEKING AND FINDING

*Keep asking, and it will be given to you. Keep searching, and you will find. Keep knocking, and the door will be opened to you. For everyone who asks receives, and the one who searches finds, and to the one who knocks, the door will be opened.*

Matthew 7:7-8 HCSB

Where is God? He is everywhere you have ever been and everywhere you will ever go. He is with you night and day; He knows your every thought; He hears your every heartbeat.

Sometimes, in the crush of your daily duties, God may seem far away. Or sometimes, when the disappointments and sorrows of life leave you brokenhearted, God may seem distant, but He is not. When you earnestly seek God, you will find Him because He is here, waiting patiently for you to reach out to Him . . . right here . . . right now.

In the space below, write down your thoughts about the need to acknowledge God's presence.

_____

_____

_____

_____

_____

_____

## BEING GENTLE WITH YOURSELF

*You're blessed when you're content with just who you are—no more, no less. That's the moment you find yourselves proud owners of everything that can't be bought.*

Matthew 5:5 MSG

God's message is clear: We must be patient with all people, beginning with that particular man or woman who stares back at us each time we gaze into the mirror. The Bible affirms the importance of self-acceptance by exhorting believers to love others as they love themselves (Matthew 22:37-40). Furthermore, the Bible teaches that when we genuinely open our hearts to Him, God accepts us just as we are. And, if He accepts us—faults and all—then who are we to believe otherwise?

Since God loves you, and since He wants the very best for you, don't you believe that He also wants you to enjoy a healthy lifestyle? Of course He does. In the space below, remind yourself of a few of the benefits you'll earn when you establish healthier habits.

## DISCIPLINE YOURSELF

*Discipline yourself for the purpose of godliness.*

1 Timothy 4:7 NASB

You live in a world where many prominent people want you to believe that dignified, self-disciplined behavior is going out of style. But don't deceive yourself: self-discipline never goes out of style. Your greatest accomplishments will probably require heaping helpings of self-discipline—which, by the way, is perfectly fine with God. After all, He knows that you're up to the task, and He has big plans for you. God will do His part to fulfill those plans, and the rest, of course, depends upon you.

Your workouts should be a source of pleasure and satisfaction, not a form of self-imposed punishment. In the space below, jot down a few ideas for making your exercise regimen more satisfying, more effective, and more fun.

_____

_____

_____

_____

_____

_____

_____

## OFFERING THANKS THAT YOU'RE RESPONSIBLE FOR THE FOODS YOU EAT

*In everything give thanks; for this is the will of God in Christ Jesus for you.*

1 Thessalonians 5:18 NKJV

It's easy to blame other people for the current state of your health. You live in a world where it's fashionable to blame food manufacturers, doctors, and fast-food restaurants, to mention but a few. Yet none of these folks force food into your mouth, and they don't force you to sit on the sofa when you should be exercising! So remember: it's your body . . . and it's your responsibility.

In the space below, thank your Creator for the gift of free will and for the ability to make choices.

_____

_____

_____

_____

_____

_____

_____

## ETERNAL PERSPECTIVE

*Our Savior Jesus poured out new life so generously. God's gift has restored our relationship with him and given us back our lives. And there's more life to come—an eternity of life!*

Titus 3:6-7 MSG

God's plans for you are not limited to the ups and downs of everyday life. Your Heavenly Father has bigger things in mind, much bigger things. Christ sacrificed His life on the cross so that we might have eternal life. This gift, freely given by God's only begotten Son, is the priceless posses-sion of everyone who accepts Him as Lord and Savior. As you struggle with the inevitable hardships and occasional disappointments of everyday life, remember that God has invited you to accept His abundance not only for today but also for all eternity. So keep things in perspective.

In the space below, write down your thoughts about the gift of eternal life.

_____

_____

_____

_____

_____

_____

## DEFEATING DISCOURAGEMENT

*The Lord is the One who will go before you. He will be with you; He will not leave you or forsake you. Do not be afraid or discouraged.*

Deuteronomy 31:8 HCSB

When we fail to meet the expectations of others, or ourselves, we may be tempted to abandon hope. Thankfully, on those cloudy days when our strength is sapped and our faith is shaken, there exists a source from which we can draw courage and wisdom. That source is God. When we seek to form a more intimate and dynamic relationship with our Creator, He renews our spirits and restores our souls. God's promise is made clear in Isaiah 40:31: "But those who wait on the Lord shall renew their strength; they shall mount up with wings like eagles, they shall run and not be weary, they shall walk and not faint" (NKJV). And upon this promise we can—and should—depend.

In the space below, write down your thoughts about God's faithfulness.

_____

_____

_____

_____

_____

## THE MASTER'S TOUCH

*Everything is possible to the one who believes.*

Mark 9:23 HCSB

When a suffering woman sought healing by simply touching the hem of His garment, Jesus turned and said, "Daughter, be of good comfort; thy faith hath made thee whole" (Matthew 9:22 KJV). We, too, can be made whole when we place our faith completely and unwaveringly in the person of Jesus Christ. If your faith is being tested to the point of breaking, know that your Savior is near. If you reach out to Him in faith, He will give you peace and heal your broken spirit. Be content to touch even the smallest fragment of the Master's garment, and He will make you whole.

In the space below, write down your thoughts about Christ's ability to make you whole.

## YOUR JOURNEY WITH GOD

*For it is God who is working among you both the willing and the working for His good purpose.*

Philippians 2:13 HCSB

Your life is a journey, and every step of the way, God is with you. Sometimes, God's plans seem unmistakably clear to you. But other times, He may lead you through the wilderness before He directs you to the Promised Land. So be patient and keep seeking His will for your life. When you do, you'll be amazed at the marvelous things that an all-powerful, all-knowing God can do. God intends to use you in wonderful, unexpected ways if you let Him. The decision to seek God's plan and to follow it is yours and yours alone. The consequences of that decision have implications that are both profound and eternal, so choose carefully.

In the space below, write down a few thoughts about God's plan for your life.

_____

_____

_____

_____

_____

_____

# BE STILL

*Be still, and know that I am God.*

Psalm 46:10 NKJV

If we seek to maintain righteous minds and compassionate hearts, we should take time each day for prayer and for meditation. We must make ourselves still in the presence of our Creator. We must quiet our minds and our hearts so that we can sense God's will, God's love, and God's Son. Has the busy pace of life robbed you of the peace that might otherwise be yours through Jesus Christ? Nothing is more important than the time you spend with your Savior. So be still and claim the inner peace that is your spiritual birthright: the peace of Jesus Christ. It is offered freely; it has been paid for in full; it is yours for the asking.

In the space below, write down a few thoughts about the importance of spending quiet time with your Savior.

_____

_____

_____

_____

_____

_____

_____

# THE POWER OF OPTIMISM

*I am able to do all things through Him who strengthens me.*

Philippians 4:13 HCSB

---

As each day unfolds, you are quite literally surrounded by more opportunities than you can count—opportunities to improve your own life and the lives of those you love. God's Word promises that you, like all of His children, possess the ability to experience earthly peace and spiritual abundance. So here's a simple tip for improving your life: expect the best, and then get busy working to achieve it. When you do, you'll not only increase the odds of achieving your goals, but you'll also have more fun along the way.

---

In the space below, write down a few thoughts about the importance of maintaining a positive attitude.

_____

_____

_____

_____

_____

_____

_____

_____

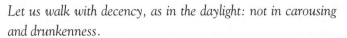

## NO MORE EXCUSES

*Let us walk with decency, as in the daylight: not in carousing and drunkenness.*

Romans 13:13 HCSB

---

All too often we are quick to proclaim ourselves "victims," and we refuse to take responsibility for our actions. So we make excuses, excuses, and more excuses—with predictably poor results. Because we humans are such creative excuse-makers, all of the really good excuses have already been taken. That's why excuses don't work—we've heard them all before. So, if you're wasting your time trying to portray yourself as a victim, or if you're trying to concoct a new and improved excuse, don't bother. Excuses don't work, and while you're inventing them, neither do you.

---

Today, think of something important that you've been putting off. Then think of the excuses you've used to avoid that responsibility. Finally, write down specific steps you can take today to finish the work you've been avoiding.

---

---

---

---

---

## DON'T BE DISCOURAGED

*Do not be afraid or discouraged, for the LORD is the one who goes before you. He will be with you; he will neither fail you nor forsake you.*

Deuteronomy 31:8 NLT

Even the best fitness plans sometimes go awry. The next time you become discouraged with the condition of your health or the direction of your day, turn your thoughts and prayers to God. He is a God of possibility, not negativity. He will help you count your blessings instead of your hardships. And then, with a renewed spirit of optimism and hope, you can rise above the disappointments and praise God for His blessings.

If life's inevitable temptations seem to be getting the best of you, try praying more often, even if many of those prayers are simply brief, "open-eyed" requests to your Father in heaven. In the space below, write down your thoughts about God's faithfulness and His plan for your life.

## IT ALL STARTS WITH GOD

*Now the God of all grace, who called you to His eternal glory in Christ Jesus, will personally restore, establish, strengthen, and support you.*

1 Peter 5:10 HCSB

Physical fitness, like every other aspect of your life, begins and ends with God. If you'd like to adopt a healthier lifestyle, God is willing to help. In fact, if you sincerely wish to create a healthier you—either physically, emotionally or spiritually—God is anxious to be your silent partner in that endeavor, but it's up to you to ask for His help.

In the space below, ask God to give you the strength and determination to exercise wisely and often.

_____

_____

_____

_____

_____

_____

_____

_____

_____

## TRUSTING HIS PROMISES

*Let us hold on to the confession of our hope without wavering, for He who promised is faithful.*

Hebrews 10:23 HCSB

For thoughtful Christians, every day begins and ends with God's Son and God's promises. When we accept Christ into our hearts, God promises us the opportunity for earthly peace and spiritual abundance. But more importantly, God promises us the priceless gift of eternal life. What do you expect from the day ahead? Are you willing to trust God completely, or are you living beneath a cloud of doubt and fear? God's Word makes it clear: you should trust Him and His promises, and when you do, you can live courageously.

In the space below, write down what God's promises mean to you.

_____

_____

_____

_____

_____

_____

_____

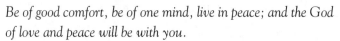

## LASTING PEACE

*Be of good comfort, be of one mind, live in peace; and the God of love and peace will be with you.*

2 Corinthians 13:11 NKJV

Have you found the lasting peace that can—and should—be yours through Jesus Christ? Or are you still chasing the illusion of "peace and happiness" that the world promises but cannot deliver?

The beautiful words of John 14:27 promise that Jesus offers peace, not as the world gives, but as He alone gives: "Peace I leave with you. My peace I give to you. I do not give to you as the world gives. Your heart must not be troubled or fearful" (HCSB). Your challenge is to accept Christ's peace into your heart and then, as best you can, to share His peace with your family and friends.

God offers peace that passes human understanding. In the space below, write down at least one thing you can do to-day to make your life less stressful and more peaceful.

_____

_____

_____

_____

_____

_____

## HAPPINESS AND HOLINESS

*Happy are the people who live at your Temple . . . . Happy are those whose strength comes from you.*

Psalm 84:4-5 NKJV

Do you seek happiness, abundance, and contentment? If so, here are some things you should do: Love God and His Son; depend upon God for strength; try, to the best of your abilities, to follow God's will; and strive to obey His Holy Word. When you do these things, you'll discover that happiness goes hand-in-hand with righteousness. The happiest people are not those who rebel against God; the happiest people are those who love God and obey His commandments.

In the space below, write down a few thoughts about happiness and holiness.

_____

_____

_____

_____

_____

_____

_____

## ASKING AND RECEIVING

*Ask, and it will be given to you; seek, and you will find; knock, and it will be opened to you. For everyone who asks receives, and he who seeks finds, and to him who knocks it will be opened.*

Matthew 7:7-8 NKJV

Jesus made it clear to His disciples: they should petition God to meet their needs. So should we. Genuine, heartfelt prayer produces powerful changes in us and in our world. When we lift our hearts to God, we open ourselves to a never-ending source of divine wisdom and infinite love. Whatever your need, no matter how great or small, pray about it and never lose hope. God is not just near; He is here, and He's perfectly capable of answering your prayers. Now, it's up to you to ask.

In the space below, write down a specific need and pray about it.

_____

_____

_____

_____

_____

_____

_____

## ABUNDANCE, NOT ANXIETY

*Cast all your anxiety on him because he cares for you.*

1 Peter 5:7 NIV

We live in a world that often breeds anxiety and fear. When we come face-to-face with tough times, we may fall prey to discouragement, doubt, or depression. But our Father in Heaven has other plans. God has promised that we may lead lives of abundance, not anxiety. In fact, His Word instructs us to "be anxious for nothing" (Philippians 4:6). But how can we put our fears to rest? By taking those fears to God and leaving them there.

In the space below, write down something that you've been anxious about. And then, turn that problem over to God and ask Him to lift any anxieties from your heart.

_____

_____

_____

_____

_____

_____

_____

_____

_____

DAY 183

# HE IS SUFFICIENT

*And He said to me, "My grace is sufficient for you, for My strength is made perfect in weakness."*

2 Corinthians 12:9 NKJV

Of this you can be certain: God is sufficient to meet your needs. The Psalmist writes, "Weeping may endure for a night, but joy comes in the morning" (Psalm 30:5 NKJV). But when we are suffering, the morning may seem very far away. It is not. God promises that He is "near to those who have a broken heart" (Psalm 34:18 NKJV). When we are troubled, we must turn to Him, and we must encourage our friends and family members to do likewise. If you are discouraged by the inevitable demands of life here on earth, be mindful of this fact: the loving heart of God is sufficient to meet any challenge . . . including yours.

In the space below, write down a few thoughts about God's sufficiency.

## KEEPING A PROPER PERSPECTIVE

*All I'm doing right now, friends, is showing how these things*
*pertain to Apollos and me so that you will learn restraint and*
*not rush into making judgments without knowing all the facts.*
*It is important to look at things from God's point of view. I*
*would rather not see you inflating or deflating reputations based*
*on mere hearsay.*

1 Corinthians 4:6 MSG

---

When the world seems to be spinning out of control, we
can regain perspective by slowing ourselves down and then
turning our thoughts and prayers toward God. Carve out
quiet moments each day to offer thanksgiving and praise
to your Creator. When you do, you can face life's complications with the wisdom, the perspective, and the power
that only He can provide.

---

Remember that your life is an integral part of God's grand
plan. So don't become unduly upset over the minor inconveniences of life, and don't worry too much about today's
setbacks—they're temporary.

---

## LOOKING BEFORE YOU LEAP

*An impulsive vow is a trap; later you'll wish you could get out of it.*

Proverbs 20:25 MSG

Are you, at times, just a little bit impulsive? If so, God wants to have a little chat with you. God's Word is clear: as believers, we are called to lead lives of discipline, diligence, moderation, and maturity. But the world often tempts us to behave impulsively. Everywhere we turn, or so it seems, we are faced with powerful temptations to binge, to overindulge, and to behave in undisciplined ways. Yet God's Word instructs us to be disciplined in our thoughts and our actions; God's Word warns us against the dangers of impulsive behavior. As believers in a just God, we should act—and react—accordingly.

In the space below, write down your thoughts about the dangers of impulsive behaviors.

_____

_____

_____

_____

_____

_____

## MODERATION IN ACTION

*Now if any of you lacks wisdom, he should ask God, who gives to all generously and without criticizing, and it will be given to him.*

James 1:5 HCSB

---

When we allow our appetites to run wild, they usually do. When we abandon moderation, we forfeit the inner peace that God offers—but does not guarantee—to His children. When we live intemperate lives, we rob ourselves of countless blessings that would have otherwise been ours. God's instructions are clear: if we seek to live wisely, we must be moderate in our appetites and disciplined in our behavior. To do otherwise is an affront to Him . . . and to ourselves.

---

Of a thousand American adults who were surveyed in a recent poll, eighty-eight percent were unable to accurately estimate how many calories they should consume each day to maintain their weight. Consequently, these adults didn't know how many calories they should consume if they wanted to lose weight. Thankfully, in these days of easy Internet information, it isn't very difficult to discover how many calories you need. In the space below, write that number.

---

---

# GOD'S PLAN FOR YOUR HEALTH

*Who are those who fear the Lord? He will show them the path they should choose. They will live in prosperity, and their children will inherit the Promised Land.*

Psalm 25:12-13 NLT

The journey toward improved health is not only a common-sense exercise in personal discipline, it is also a spiritual journey ordained by our Creator. God does not intend that we abuse our bodies by giving in to excessive appetites or to slothful behavior. To the contrary, God has instructed us to protect our physical bodies to the greatest extent we can. When you make the decision to seek God's will for your life, then you will contemplate His Word, and you will be watchful for His signs. And then, as you go about your daily activities, you will keep your eyes and ears open, as well as your heart.

In the space below, write some of your thoughts about God's plan for your spiritual, physical, and emotional health.

_____

_____

_____

_____

_____

## VALUE-BASED DECISIONS

*We encouraged, comforted, and implored each one of you to walk worthy of God, who calls you into His own kingdom and glory.*

1 Thessalonians 2:12 HCSB

Society seeks to impose its set of values upon you, however these values are often contrary to God's Word (and thus contrary to your own best interests). The world makes promises that it simply cannot fulfill. It promises happiness, contentment, prosperity, and abundance. But genuine abundance is not a by-product of possessions or status; it is a by-product of your thoughts, your actions, and your relationship with God. The world's promises are incomplete and deceptive; God's promises are unfailing. Your challenge, then, is to build your value system upon the firm foundation of God's promises . . . nothing else will suffice.

In the space below, write down at least five values that you intend to live by.

_____

_____

_____

_____

_____

# THE SOURCE OF STRENGTH

*And He said to me, "My grace is sufficient for you, for My strength is made perfect in weakness."*

2 Corinthians 12:9 NKJV

Are you an energized Christian? You should be. But if you're not, you must seek strength and renewal from the source that will never fail: that source, of course, is your Heavenly Father. And rest assured—when you sincerely petition Him, He will give you all the strength you need to live victoriously for Him. Have you "tapped in" to the power of God? Have you turned your life and your heart over to Him, or are you muddling along under your own power? The answer to this question will determine the quality of your life here on earth and the destiny of your life throughout all eternity. So start tapping in—and remember that when it comes to strength, God is the Ultimate Source.

Today, jot down a few ways that you can tap into God's strength: consider prayer, worship, and praise, for starters.

_____

_____

_____

_____

_____

# EMOTIONS:
## WHO'S IN CHARGE OF YOURS?

*For this very reason, make every effort to supplement your faith with goodness, goodness with knowledge, knowledge with self-control, self-control with endurance, endurance with godliness.*

2 Peter 1:5-6 HCSB

When anger or anxiety separates us from the spiritual blessings that God has in store, we must rethink our priorities and renew our faith. And we must place faith above feelings. Human emotions are highly variable, decidedly unpredictable, and often unreliable. So we must learn to live by faith, not by the ups and downs of our own emotional roller coasters.

Your emotions are powerful things, but they shouldn't rule your life. Your life should be ruled by God. Think about when you've lost control over your emotions and write down some ways you can calm yourself down before you do something rash the next time.

_____

_____

_____

_____

_____

## GOD IS LOVE

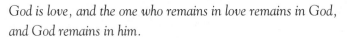

*God is love, and the one who remains in love remains in God, and God remains in him.*

1 John 4:16 HCSB

The Bible makes this promise: God is love. It's a sweeping statement, a profoundly important description of what God is and how God works. God's love is perfect. When we open our hearts to His perfect love, we are touched by the Creator's hand, and we are transformed. Today, even if you can only carve out a few quiet moments, offer sincere prayers of thanksgiving to your Creator. He loves you now and throughout all eternity. Open your heart to His presence and His love.

In the space below, write down your thoughts about God's love for you and your family.

_____

_____

_____

_____

_____

_____

_____

## GENTLENESS OF SPIRIT

*Let your gentleness be evident to all. The Lord is near.*

Philippians 4:5 NIV

In a letter to the Christians at Philippi, Paul instructed his friends to make their gentleness evident to all. But, even for the most dedicated Christians, it is sometimes difficult to be gentle. As fallible human beings, we are subject to the normal frustrations of daily life, and when we are, we are tempted to strike out in anger. As long as you live here on earth, you will face countless opportunities to lose your temper over small, relatively insignificant events. When you are tempted to lose your temper over the minor inconveniences of life, don't. Turn away from anger and turn instead to God; when you do, He will fill you with a loving spirit that will help you deal gently and generously with others.

In the space below, write down your thoughts about the rewards of being a gentle and generous person.

## BE A CHEERFUL CHRISTIAN

*A cheerful heart has a continual feast.*

Proverbs 15:15 HCSB

Cheerfulness is its own reward—but not its only reward. Are you a cheerful Christian? You should be! After all, God's gifts to you include, but are not limited to, infinite love and eternal life. Billy Graham wrote, "Christ can put a spring in your step and a thrill in your heart. Optimism and cheerfulness are products of knowing Christ." So today, and every day, celebrate God's gifts and God's Son with a smile on your lips and joy in your heart. The world needs all the good cheer—and Good News—it can get.

Write down your thoughts about the good things that happen when you smile.

_____

_____

_____

_____

_____

_____

_____

## REBELLION INVITES DISASTER

*You must follow the Lord your God and fear Him. You must keep His commands and listen to His voice; you must worship Him and remain faithful to Him.*

Deuteronomy 13:4 HCSB

The English clergyman Thomas Fuller observed, "He does not believe who does not live according to his beliefs." These words are most certainly true. We may proclaim our beliefs to our hearts' content, but our proclamations will mean nothing unless we accompany our words with deeds that match. The sermons that we live are far more compelling than the ones we preach. So today, do whatever you can to ensure that your thoughts and your deeds are pleasing to your Creator. Because you will, at some point in the future, be called to account for your actions.

Be honest with yourself as you consider ways that you have, in the last few days, disobeyed God. Then, write down some specific ways that you can be more obedient today.

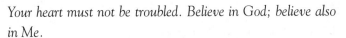

## BEYOND WORRY

*Your heart must not be troubled. Believe in God; believe also in Me.*

John 14:1 HCSB

Because we are fallible human beings, we worry. Even though we, as Christians, have the promise of God's love and protection, we find ourselves fretting over the countless details of everyday life.

If you are like most women, you may, on occasion, find yourself worrying about health, about finances, about safety, about relationships, about family, and about countless other challenges of life, some great and some small. Where is the best place to take your worries? Take them to God. Take your troubles to Him, and your fears, and your sorrows. And remember: God is trustworthy…and you are protected.

In the space below, write down your thoughts about the futility of worry.

_____

_____

_____

_____

_____

_____

## STUDYING HIS WORD

*Man shall not live by bread alone, but by every word that proceeds from the mouth of God.*

Matthew 4:4 NKJV

George Mueller observed, "The vigor of our spiritual lives will be in exact proportion to the place held by the Bible in our lives and in our thoughts." Think of it like this: the more you use your Bible, the more God will use you. God's Word can be a roadmap to a place of righteousness and abundance. Make it your roadmap. God's wisdom can be a light to guide your steps. Claim it as your light today, tomorrow, and every day of your life—and then walk confidently in the footsteps of God's only begotten Son.

In the space below, write down a favorite Bible verse, and then try your best to memorize it today.

_____

_____

_____

_____

_____

_____

_____

## THE GIFT OF GOD'S GRACE

*But God, who is abundant in mercy, because of His great love that He had for us, made us alive with the Messiah even though we were dead in trespasses. By grace you are saved!*

Ephesians 2:4-5 HCSB

We have received countless gifts from God, but none can compare with the gift of salvation. When we accept Christ into our hearts, we are saved by God's grace. We are saved, not because of our good deeds, but because of our faith in Christ. God's grace is the ultimate gift, and we owe Him the ultimate in thanksgiving. Let us praise the Creator for His priceless gift, and let us share the Good News with all who cross our paths. We return our Father's love by accepting His grace and by sharing His message and His love. When we do, we are blessed here on earth and throughout all eternity.

God's grace isn't earned, but freely given—what an amazing, humbling gift. In the space below, thank God for His incredible gift.

## PHYSICAL FITNESS DAY BY DAY

*Dear friend, I pray that you may prosper in every way and be in good health, just as your soul prospers.*

3 John 1:2 HCSB

The road to poor health is paved with good intentions. Until you make exercise a high priority in your life, your good intentions will soon give way to old habits. So give your exercise regimen a position of high standing on your daily to-do list. And while you're at it, remember that your journey with God unfolds day by day, and that's precisely how your journey to an improved state of physical fitness must also unfold: moment by moment, day by day, year by year.

Fitness is a journey, not a destination. Achieving physical fitness and maintaining it is a seven-day-a-week assignment. In the space below, write down a few thoughts about the current state of your physical health, and ways you might improve it.

_____

_____

_____

_____

_____

_____

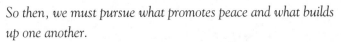

# PATS ON THE BACK

*So then, we must pursue what promotes peace and what builds up one another.*

Romans 14:19 HCSB

---

Life is a team sport, and all of us need occasional pats on the back from our teammates. In the book of Ephesians, Paul writes, "Do not let any unwholesome talk come out of your mouths, but only what is helpful for building others up according to their needs, that it may benefit those who listen" (4:29 NIV). Paul reminds us that when we choose our words carefully, we can have a powerful impact on those around us.

Since we don't always know who needs our help, the best strategy is to encourage all the people who cross our paths. So today, be a world-class source of encouragement to everyone you meet. Never has the need been greater.

---

In the space below, write down the names of several friends who might benefit from a pat on the back or an encouraging word.

---

---

---

---

---

# YOUR BODY NEEDS HEALTHY FOODS

*Don't you know that you are God's sanctuary and that the Spirit of God lives in you?*

1 Corinthians 3:16 HCSB

We live in a junk-food society, but you shouldn't let your house become junk-food heaven. So do your loved ones a favor: make your home a haven of healthy foods. And re-member, it's never too soon to teach your family good hab-its . . . and that includes the good habit of sensible eating.

In the space below, make a list of some foods that you and your family should eliminate from your diet.

_____

_____

_____

_____

_____

_____

_____

_____

_____

_____

## PERSPECTIVE AND BALANCE

*Come to Me, all you who labor and are heavy laden, and I will give you rest. Take My yoke upon you and learn from Me, for I am gentle and lowly in heart, and you will find rest for your souls. For My yoke is easy and My burden is light.*

Matthew 11:28-30 NKJV

Sometimes, amid the demands of daily life, we lose perspective. Life seems out of balance, and the pressures of everyday living seem overwhelming. What's needed is a fresh perspective, a restored sense of balance . . . and God. When you call upon the Lord and prayerfully seek His will, He will give you wisdom and perspective. When you make God's priorities your priorities, He will direct your steps and calm your fears. So today and every day hereafter, pray for a sense of balance and perspective. And remember: your thoughts are intensely powerful things, so handle them with care.

Life is a balancing act. In the space below, ask God to help you find a balance that is pleasing to Him.

_____

_____

_____

_____

_____

# GOD'S GUIDANCE

*Those who are blessed by Him will inherit the land.*

Psalm 37:22 HCSB

God wants us to care for our bodies, but He does not require us to do so. We are creatures of free will, able to make decisions on our own. When we stray from God's commandments, we invite bitter consequences. But, when we genuinely seek His will, He touches our hearts and leads us on the path of His choosing. Will you trust God to guide your steps? You should. When you entrust your life to Him completely and without reservation, God will give you the strength to meet any challenge, the courage to face any trial, and the wisdom to live in His righteousness and in His peace. So trust Him today and seek His guidance. When you do, your next step will be the right one.

In the space below, write down your thoughts about the role that God's instruction does play, and should play, in your life.

_____

_____

_____

_____

_____

## WE ARE ALL ROLE MODELS

*Therefore, we are ambassadors for Christ; certain that God is appealing through us, we plead on Christ's behalf, "Be reconciled to God."*

2 Corinthians 5:20 HCSB

Whether we like it or not, all of us are role models. Our friends and family members watch our actions and, as followers of Christ, we are obliged to act accordingly.

What kind of example are you? Are you the kind of person whose life serves as a genuine example of moderation and righteousness? If so, you are not only blessed by God, you are also a powerful force for good in a world that desperately needs positive influences such as yours.

In the space below, write down the names of family members and friends who look to your example.

_____

_____

_____

_____

_____

_____

_____

# A WALK WITH GOD

*For I have given you an example that you also should do just as
I have done for you.*

John 13:15 HCSB

Each day, we are confronted with countless opportunities
to serve God and to follow in the footsteps of His Son.
When we do, our Heavenly Father guides our steps and
blesses our endeavors. As citizens of a fast-changing world,
we face challenges that sometimes leave us feeling over-
worked, over-committed, and overwhelmed. But God has
different plans for us. He intends that we slow down long
enough to praise Him and to glorify His Son. When we do,
He lifts our spirits and enriches our lives.

In the space below, write down your thoughts about following Christ.

_____

_____

_____

_____

_____

_____

_____

_____

## OUR ADDICTIVE SOCIETY

*So let God work his will in you. Yell a loud no to the Devil and watch him scamper. Say a quiet yes to God and he'll be there in no time. Quit dabbling in sin. Purify your inner life. Quit playing the field.*

James 4:7-8 MSG

Ours is a highly addictive society. Why? Simple: supply and demand. The supply of addictive substances continues to grow; the affordability and availability of these substances makes them highly attractive to consumers; and the overall demand for addictive substances has increased as more and more users have become addicted to an ever-expanding array of substances and compulsions.

You know people who are full-blown addicts—probably lots of people. Your challenge is to make sure that you're not one of them.

In the space below, ask God to give you the wisdom to recognize addictive behaviors and the strength to avoid them.

_____

_____

_____

_____

_____

## EXPECTING THE BEST

*Set your minds on what is above, not on what is on the earth.*

Colossians 3:2 HCSB

---

When we accept Christ into our hearts, God promises us the opportunity for earthly peace and spiritual abundance. But more importantly, God promises us the priceless gift of eternal life. As we face the inevitable challenges of life-here-on-earth, we must arm ourselves with the promises of God's Holy Word. When we do, we can expect the best, not only for the day ahead, but also for all eternity.

---

In the space below, write down your thoughts about God's promises and your fitness.

_____

_____

_____

_____

_____

_____

_____

_____

_____

_____

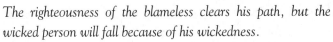

# THE BEST POLICY

*The righteousness of the blameless clears his path, but the wicked person will fall because of his wickedness.*

Proverbs 11:5 HCSB

From the time we are children, we are taught that honesty is the best policy, but sometimes, being honest is hard. So, we convince ourselves that it's alright to tell "little white lies." But there's a problem: Little white lies tend to grow up, and when they do, they cause havoc and pain in our lives. Honesty is not just the best policy, it is God's policy, pure and simple. And if we are to be servants worthy of our Savior, Jesus Christ, we must avoid all lies, white or otherwise. So, if you're tempted to sow the seeds of deception (perhaps in the form of a "harmless" white lie), resist that temptation.

In the space below, write down your thoughts about the rewards of honesty and the dangers of dishonesty.

_____

_____

_____

_____

_____

_____

## HONORING GOD

*Honor GOD with everything you own; give him the first and the best. Your barns will burst, your wine vats will brim over.*

Proverbs 3:9-10 MSG

Whom will you choose to honor today? If you honor God and place Him at the center of your life, every day is a cause for celebration. But if you fail to honor your Heavenly Father, you're asking for trouble, and lots of it. At times, your life is probably hectic, demanding, and complicated. When the demands of life leave you rushing from place to place with scarcely a moment to spare, you may fail to pause and thank your Creator for the blessings He has bestowed upon you. But that's a big mistake. So don't just honor God on Sunday morning. Praise Him all day long, every day, for as long as you live.

In the space below, write down your thoughts about honoring God with your faith and your fitness.

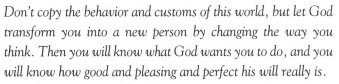

# A DANGEROUS SOCIETY AND YOUR SPIRITUAL HEALTH

*Don't copy the behavior and customs of this world, but let God transform you into a new person by changing the way you think. Then you will know what God wants you to do, and you will know how good and pleasing and perfect his will really is.*

Romans 12:2 NLT

If you find yourself frustrated by the unrealistic demands of others (or by unrealistic pressures of the self-imposed variety), it's time to ask yourself who you're trying to impress, and why. Your first responsibility is to the Heavenly Father who created you and to the Son who saved you. Then, you bear a powerful responsibility to be true to yourself. And of course you owe debts of gratitude to friends and family members. But, when it comes to meeting society's unrealistic expectations, forget it! Those expectations aren't just unrealistic; they're detrimental to your spiritual health.

In the space below, ask God to protect you against the dangers of the world.

_____

_____

_____

_____

_____

## THE SEARCH FOR ENCOURAGEMENT

*As iron sharpens iron, a friend sharpens a friend.*

Proverbs 27:17 NLT

If you're trying to reshape your physique or your life, don't try to do it alone. Ask for the support and encouragement of your family members and friends. You'll improve your odds of success if you enlist your own cheering section.

In the space below, make a list of your most encouraging family members and friends.

_____

_____

_____

_____

_____

_____

_____

_____

_____

_____

## BUILD THE CHURCH OF GOD

*Be on guard for yourselves and for all the flock, among whom
the Holy Spirit has appointed you as overseers, to shepherd the
church of God, which He purchased with His own blood.*

Acts 20:28 HCSB

If you want to start building a healthier, happier life, the
church is a wonderful place to do it. Are you an active,
contributing, member of your local fellowship? The answer to this simple question will have a profound impact
on the direction of your spiritual journey and the content
of your character.

God intends for you to be actively involved in His church.
In the space below, evaluate the level of your participation
at church.

## DURING DIFFICULT DAYS

*We also have joy with our troubles, because we know that these troubles produce patience. And patience produces character, and character produces hope.*

Romans 5:3-4 NCV

When we find ourselves overtaken by the minor frustrations of life, we must catch ourselves, take a deep breath, and lift our thoughts upward. Although we are here on earth struggling to rise above the distractions of the day, we need never struggle alone. God is here—eternally and faithfully, with infinite patience and love—and, if we reach out to Him, He will restore perspective and peace to our souls. If you become discouraged with the direction of your day or your life, lift your thoughts and prayers to Him. He will guide you through your difficulties and beyond.

In the space below, write down your thoughts about God's protection.

## REMEMBER THE SABBATH

*Remember the Sabbath day, to keep it holy.*

Exodus 20:8 NKJV

How does your family observe the Lord's day? When church is over, do you treat Sunday like any other day of the week? If so, it's time to think long and hard about your family's schedule and your family's priorities. And if you've been treating Sunday as just another day, it's time to break that habit. When Sunday rolls around, don't try to fill every spare moment. Take time to rest . . . Father's orders!

The Sabbath is unlike the other six days of the week, and it's up to you to treat it that way. In the space below, write down ways you can honor God on the Sabbath.

_____

_____

_____

_____

_____

_____

_____

_____

## THE POWER OF FAITH

*Believe in the Lord your God, and you will be established;*
*believe in His prophets, and you will succeed.*

2 Chronicles 20:20 HCSB

When you place your faith, your trust, indeed your life in the hands of Christ Jesus, you'll be amazed at the marvelous things He can do with you and through you. So strengthen your faith through praise, through worship, through Bible study, and through prayer. And trust God's plans. With Him, all things are possible, and He stands ready to open a world of possibilities to you . . . if you have faith.

In the space below, write down your thoughts about the power of faith.

_____

_____

_____

_____

_____

_____

_____

_____

## ASK HIM TO STRENGTHEN YOU

*Is anything too hard for the LORD?*

Genesis 18:14 KJV

If you want to strengthen your faith or improve your fitness, God can help. He is a God of infinite possibilities. But sometimes, because of limited faith and limited understanding, we wrongly assume that God cannot or will not intervene in the affairs of mankind. Such assumptions are simply wrong. Are you afraid to ask God to do big things in your life? If so, it's time to abandon your doubts and reclaim your faith in God's promises. God's Holy Word makes it clear: absolutely nothing is impossible for the Lord. Your challenge, as a believer, is to take God at His word, and to expect the miraculous.

In the space below, ask God to help you reach a specific short-term goal.

_____

_____

_____

_____

_____

_____

## GOD'S TIMETABLE

*Humble yourselves therefore under the mighty hand of God, so that He may exalt you in due time, casting all your care upon Him, because He cares about you.*

1 Peter 5:6-7 HCSB

Sometimes, the hardest thing to do is to wait. This is especially true when we're in a hurry and when we want things to happen now, if not sooner! But God's plan does not always happen in the way that we would like or at the time of our own choosing. Our task—as believing Christians who trust in a benevolent, all knowing Father—is to wait patiently for God to reveal Himself. We human beings are, by nature, impatient. We know what we want, and we know exactly when we want it: RIGHT NOW! But, God knows better. He has created a world that unfolds according to His own timetable, not ours . . . thank goodness!

In the space below, write down your thoughts about God's perfect timing.

_____

_____

_____

_____

_____

_____

## LIGHTING THE PATH

*Your word is a lamp to my feet and a light to my path.*

Psalm 119:105 NKJV

Are you a woman who trusts God's Word without reservation? Hopefully so, because the Bible is unlike any other book—it is a guidebook for life here on earth and for life eternal. The Psalmist describes God's Word as, "a light to my path." Is the Bible your lamp? If not, you are depriving yourself of a priceless gift from the Creator. Vance Havner observed, "It takes calm, thoughtful, prayerful meditation on the Word to extract its deepest nourishment." How true. God's Word can be a light to guide your steps. Claim it as your light today, tomorrow, and every day of your life—and then walk confidently in the footsteps of God's only begotten Son.

In the space below, write down your thoughts about ways that God's promises can impact your faith and your fitness.

_____

_____

_____

_____

_____

_____

_____

## SEEKING HIS WILL

*Teach me to do Your will, for You are my God; Your Spirit is good. Lead me in the land of uprightness.*

Psalm 143:10 NKJV

God has a plan for our world and our lives. God does not do things by accident; He is willful and intentional. Unfortunately for us, we cannot always understand the will of God. Why? Because we are mortal beings with limited understanding. Although we cannot fully comprehend the will of God, we should always trust the will of God. As this day unfolds, seek God's will and obey His Word. When you entrust your life to Him without reservation, He will give you the courage meet any challenge, the strength to endure any trial, and the wisdom to live in His righteousness and in His peace.

In the space below, write down your thoughts about your willingness to seek and follow God's will.

_____

_____

_____

_____

_____

_____

_____

## TO JUDGE OR NOT TO JUDGE

*When they persisted in questioning Him, He stood up and said to them, "The one without sin among you should be the first to throw a stone at her."*

John 8:7 HCSB

The warning of Matthew 7:1 is clear: "Judge not, that ye be not judged" (KJV). Yet even the most devoted Christians may fall prey to a powerful yet subtle temptation: the temptation to judge others. But as obedient followers of Christ, we are commanded to refrain from such behavior. As Jesus came upon a young woman who had been condemned by the Pharisees, He spoke not only to the crowd that was gathered there, but also to all generations when He warned, "He that is without sin among you, let him first cast a stone at her" (John 8:7 KJV). Christ's message is clear, and it applies not only to the Pharisees of ancient times, but also to us.

In the space below, write down your thoughts about the dangers of judging other people.

_____

_____

_____

_____

_____

## MAKING PEACE WITH YOUR PAST

*Forget about what's happened; don't keep going over old history. Be alert, be present. I'm about to do something brand-new. It's bursting out! Don't you see it? There it is! I'm making a road through the desert, rivers in the badlands.*

Isaiah 43:18–19 MSG

Have you made peace with your past? If so, congratulations. But, if you are mired in the quicksand of regret, it's time to plan your escape. How can you do so? By accepting what has been and by trusting God for what will be. Because you are human, you may be slow to forget yesterday's disappointments. But, if you sincerely seek to focus your hopes and energies on the future, then you must find ways to accept the past. When you do, you can then turn your thoughts to the wondrous promises of God and the glorious future that He has in store for you.

In the space below, write down something you need to forget or someone you need to forgive.

_____

_____

_____

_____

_____

# GOD'S GUIDANCE AND YOUR PATH

*Trust in the LORD with all your heart; do not depend on your own understanding. Seek his will in all you do, and he will direct your paths.*

Proverbs 3:5-6 NLT

As you prayerfully consider the path that God intends for you to take, here are things you should do: You should study His Word and be ever-watchful for His signs. You should associate with fellow believers who will encourage your spiritual growth. You should listen carefully to that inner voice that speaks to you in the quiet moments of your daily devotionals. You can rest assured that God intends to use you in wonderful, unexpected ways. Your challenge is to watch, to listen, to learn . . . and to follow.

In the space below, write down your thoughts about the path you're on today and the path you believe God wants you to take tomorrow.

_____

_____

_____

_____

_____

_____

## STANDING UP FOR YOUR FAITH

*Be alert, stand firm in the faith, be brave and strong.*

1 Corinthians 16:13 HCSB

Are you a person whose faith is obvious to your family and to the world? Hopefully so. God intends for you to stand up and be counted for Him. Genuine faith is never meant to be locked up in the heart of a believer; to the contrary, it is meant to be shared. And the best day to share the Good News is today.

In the space below, make a few notes about your own personal testimony.

_____

_____

_____

_____

_____

_____

_____

_____

_____

_____

_____

## HIS TRANSFORMING POWER

*Your old sinful self has died, and your new life is kept with Christ in God.*

Colossians 3:3 NCV

God's hand has the power to transform your fitness, your faith, and your life. Your task is to accept Christ's grace with a humble, thankful heart as you receive the "new life" that can be yours through Him. Do you desire to improve some aspect of your life? If so, don't expect changing circumstances to miraculously transform you into the person you want to become. Transformation starts with God, and it starts in the quiet corners of a willing human heart—like yours.

In the space below, make a few notes about your own personal transformation.

_____

_____

_____

_____

_____

_____

_____

# CONSIDER THE POSSIBILITIES

*But Jesus looked at them and said, "With men this is impossible,
but with God all things are possible."*

Matthew 19:26 HCSB

If you find yourself enduring difficult circumstances, perhaps it's time for an extreme intellectual makeover—it's
time to focus more on your strengths and opportunities,
and less on the challenges that confront you. One more
thing: it's time to put a little more faith in God. Every
day is filled with opportunities to grow, to serve, and to
share. But if you are entangled in a web of negativity, you
may overlook the blessings that God has scattered along
your path. So don't give in to pessimism, to doubt, or to
cynicism. Instead, keep your eyes upon the possibilities,
fix your heart upon God, do your best, and let Him handle
the rest.

In the space below, write down the most important steps
you can take to improve your physical, spiritual, or emotional health today.

_____

_____

_____

_____

_____

## LIVING ON PURPOSE

*He is the image of the invisible God, the firstborn over all creation; because by Him everything was created, in heaven and on earth, the visible and the invisible, whether thrones or dominions or rulers or authorities—all things have been created through Him and for Him.*

Colossians 1:15-16 HCSB

---

"What did God put me here to do?" If you're like most people, you've asked yourself that question on many occasions. If you don't have a clear plan for the next step of your life's journey, you may rest assured that God does.

God has a plan for the universe, and He has a plan for you. He understands that plan as thoroughly and completely as He knows you. If you seek God's will earnestly and prayerfully, He will make His plans known to you in His own time and in His own way.

---

Perhaps you're in a hurry to understand God's unfolding plan for your life. If so, remember that God operates according to a perfect timetable. Jot down ways you can show others how God lives in you.

_____

_____

_____

_____

_____

# YOUR PHYSICAL AND SPIRITUAL FITNESS: WHO'S IN CHARGE?

*But seek ye first the kingdom of God, and his righteousness; and all these things shall be added unto you.*

Matthew 6:33 KJV

One of the surest ways to improve your health and your life—and the best way—is to do it with God as your partner. When you put God first in every aspect of your life, you'll be comforted by the knowledge that His wisdom is the ultimate wisdom and that His plans are the right plans for you. When you put God first, your outlook will change, your priorities will change, your behaviors will change, and your health will change. When you put Him first, you'll experience the genuine peace and lasting comfort that only He can give.

God deserves first place in your life and you deserve the experience of putting Him there. In the space below, write down your thoughts on putting God first.

_____

_____

_____

_____

_____

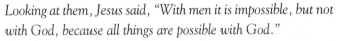

## BIG DREAMS

*Looking at them, Jesus said, "With men it is impossible, but not with God, because all things are possible with God."*

Mark 10:27 HCSB

Are you willing to entertain the possibility that God has big plans in store for you? Hopefully so. Yet sometimes, especially if you've recently experienced a life-altering disappointment, you may find it difficult to envision a brighter future for yourself and your family. If so, it's time to reconsider your own capabilities . . . and God's.

Your Heavenly Father created you with unique gifts and untapped talents; your job is to tap them. When you do, you'll begin to feel an increasing sense of confidence in yourself and in your future.

In the space below, write down a dream so big that you can only accomplish it with God's help.

_____

_____

_____

_____

_____

_____

_____

## A ONE-OF-A-KIND TREASURE

*Every word of God is pure; He is a shield to those who put their trust in Him.*

Proverbs 30:5 NKJV

Is Bible study a high priority for you? The answer to this simple question will determine, to a surprising extent, the quality of your life and the direction of your faith.

As you establish priorities for life, you must decide whether God's Word will be a bright spotlight that guides your path every day or a tiny nightlight that occasionally flickers in the dark. The decision to study the Bible—or not—is yours and yours alone. But make no mistake: how you choose to use your Bible will have a profound impact on you and your loved ones.

Today, write about the role that the Bible plays in your everyday life.

_____

_____

_____

_____

_____

_____

_____

## HOLDING ON TO HOPE

*We have this hope—like a sure and firm anchor of the soul—*
*that enters the inner sanctuary behind the curtain.*

Hebrews 6:19 HCSB

If you find yourself falling into the spiritual traps of worry and discouragement, seek the healing touch of Jesus and the encouraging words of fellow Christians. It was Christ who promised, "These things I have spoken unto you, that in me ye might have peace. In the world ye shall have tribulation: but be of good cheer; I have overcome the world" (John 16:33 KJV). This world can be a place of trials and tribulations, but as believers, we are secure. God has promised us peace, joy, and eternal life. And, of course, God keeps His promises today, tomorrow, and forever.

In the space below, make a list of restaurants that you and your family should probably avoid.

_____

_____

_____

_____

_____

_____

## SENSIBLE DINING

*Their end is destruction; their god is their stomach; their glory is in their shame. They are focused on earthly things.*

Philippians 3:19 HCSB

In the good old days, dining out used to be an occasional treat for most families. Now, it's more of an everyday occurrence. But there's a catch: most restaurants aim for taste first, price second, and health a distant third. But you should think health first. So the next time you head out for a burger, a bagel, or any other fast food, take a minute to read the fine print that's usually posted on the wall. You may find out that the healthy-sounding treat is actually a calorie-bomb in disguise.

In the space below, write down some your favorite fast-foods. Then, get online and see what you're really eating.

_____

_____

_____

_____

_____

_____

_____

## CALMNESS IN CHAOS

*Thou wilt keep him in perfect peace, whose mind is stayed on thee.*

Isaiah 26:3 KJV

---

Peace can be a scarce commodity in a demanding world. How, then, can we find the peace that we so desperately desire? By turning our days and our lives over to God. Does peace seem to be a distant promise? It is not. God's peace is available to you this very moment if you place absolute trust in Him. Elisabeth Elliot writes, "If my life is surrendered to God, all is well. Let me not grab it back, as though it were in peril in His hand but would be safer in mine!" Today, let go of your concerns by turning them over to God. Trust Him in the present moment, and accept His peace . . . in the present moment.

---

In the space below, write down your thoughts about the peace that passes all understanding: God's peace.

---

---

---

---

---

## IT PAYS TO BE MODERATE

*Do you like honey? Don't eat too much of it, or it will make you sick!*

Proverbs 25:16 NLT

If we are wise, we must learn to temper our appetites, our desires, and our impulses. When we do, we are blessed, in part, because God has created a world in which temperance is rewarded and intemperance is inevitably punished. Would you like to improve your fitness and your life? If so, put the breaks on your appetite because moderation pays, but excess doesn't.

In the space below, write down your thoughts on the rewards of controlling your appetite.

_____

_____

_____

_____

_____

_____

_____

_____

## BE CHEERFUL

*Be cheerful no matter what; pray all the time; thank God no matter what happens. This is the way God wants you who belong to Christ Jesus to live.*

1 Thessalonians 5:16-18 MSG

Few things in life are more sad, or, for that matter, more absurd, than a grumpy Christian. Christ promises us lives of abundance and joy, but He does not force His joy upon us. We must claim His joy for ourselves, and when we do, Jesus, in turn, fills our spirits with His power and His love. How can we receive from Christ the joy that is rightfully ours? By giving Him what is rightfully His: our hearts and our souls. When we place Jesus at the center of our lives and trust Him as our personal Savior, He will transform us. Then we, as God's children, can share Christ's joy and His message with a world that needs both.

In the space below, list at least five things you have to be cheerful about.

_____

_____

_____

_____

_____

# OBEDIENCE IS A WAY TO WORSHIP

*Therefore, everyone who hears these words of Mine and acts on them will be like a sensible man who built his house on the rock. The rain fell, the rivers rose, and the winds blew and pounded that house. Yet it didn't collapse, because its foundation was on the rock.*

Matthew 7:24-25 HCSB

Every day provides opportunities to put God where He belongs: at the center of our lives. When we do so, we worship not just with our words, but also with our deeds. And one way that we can honor our Heavenly Father is by treating our bodies with care and respect. The Bible makes it clear: "Your body is the temple of the Holy Spirit" (1 Corinthians 6:19 NLT). Treat it that way. And consider your fitness regimen to be one way—a very important way—of worshipping God.

In the space below, write down something that God is placing on your heart.

_____

_____

_____

_____

_____

## WISDOM EVERY MORNING

*Morning by morning he wakens me and opens my understanding to his will. The Sovereign Lord has spoken to me, and I have listened.*

Isaiah 50:4-5 NLT

Need wisdom? Then have a daily planning session with God. A regularly scheduled time of prayer, Bible reading, and meditation can help you prioritize your day and your life. And what if you're simply too busy to spend five or ten minutes with God? If so, it's time to reorder your priorities.

In the space below, write down a few of the rewards you receive when you obey God.

_____

_____

_____

_____

_____

_____

_____

_____

_____

## CELEBRATING OTHERS

*Therefore encourage one another and build each other up as you are already doing.*

1 Thessalonians 5:11 HCSB

---

Do you delight in the victories of others? You should. Each day provides countless opportunities to encourage others and to praise their good works. When you do so, you not only spread seeds of joy and happiness, you also obey the commandments of God's Holy Word. As Christians, we are called upon to spread the Good News of Christ, and we are also called to spread a message of encouragement and hope to the world. So, let us be cheerful Christians with smiles on our faces and encouraging words on our lips. By blessing others, we also bless ourselves, and, at the same time, we do honor to the One who gave His life for us.

---

In the space below, write down your thoughts about the value of encouragement.

---

_____

_____

_____

_____

_____

_____

## GOD'S ALLY

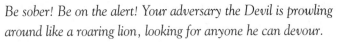

*Be sober! Be on the alert! Your adversary the Devil is prowling around like a roaring lion, looking for anyone he can devour.*

1 Peter 5:8 HCSB

Nineteenth-century clergyman Edwin Hubbel Chapin warned, "Neutral people are the devil's allies." His words were true then, and they're true now. Neutrality in the face of evil is a sin. Yet all too often, we fail to fight evil, not because we are neutral, but because we are shortsighted: we don't fight the devil because we don't recognize his handiwork. When we observe life objectively, and when we do so with eyes and hearts that are attuned to God's Holy Word, we can no longer be neutral believers. And when we are no longer neutral, God rejoices while the devil despairs.

In the space below, describe some of the evils that the popular media not only accepts but endorses.

_____

_____

_____

_____

_____

## ULTIMATE PROTECTION

*What time I am afraid, I will trust in thee.*

Psalm 56:3 KJV

God has promised to protect us, and He intends to fulfill His promise. In a world filled with dangers and temptations, God is the ultimate armor. In a world filled with misleading messages, God's Word is the ultimate truth. In a world filled with more frustrations than we can count, God's Son offers the ultimate peace. Will you accept God's peace and wear God's armor against the dangers of our world? Hopefully so, because when you do, you can live courageously, knowing that you possess the ultimate protection: God's unfailing love for you.

In the space below, write down your thoughts about God's protection.

_____

_____

_____

_____

_____

_____

_____

## STRENGTH FOR TODAY

*I can do all things through Christ which strengtheneth me.*

Philippians 4:13 KJV

Have you made God the cornerstone of your life, or is He relegated to a few hours on Sunday morning? Have you genuinely allowed God to reign over every corner of your heart, or have you attempted to place Him in a spiritual compartment? The answer to these questions will determine the direction of your day and your life. God loves you. Welcome Him in and allow Him to rule. And then, accept the peace, the strength, the protection, and the abundance that only God can give.

If you're trying to improve your fitness, or any other aspect of your life, don't spend endless hours fretting over your fate. Simply seek God's counsel and get busy. In the space below, write down your thoughts about God's willingness to provide the strength you need to meet your goals.

_____

_____

_____

_____

_____

## NO SHORTCUTS

*Go to the ant, you sluggard! Consider her ways and be wise, which, having no captain, overseer or ruler, provides her supplies in the summer, and gathers her food in the harvest. How long will you slumber, O sluggard? When will you rise from your sleep?*

Proverbs 6:6-9 NKJV

Do you have important goals you've yet to accomplish? Here's a time-tested formula for success: have faith in God and do the work. It has been said that there are no short-cuts to any place worth going, and those words apply to your physical fitness, too. There are simply no shortcuts to a healthy lifestyle.

In the space below, review your most important goals and grade yourself on the amount of energy you've invested in accomplishing those goals.

_____

_____

_____

_____

_____

_____

_____

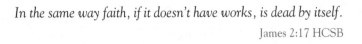

# FAITH THAT WORKS

*In the same way faith, if it doesn't have works, is dead by itself.*

James 2:17 HCSB

Corrie ten Boom advised, "Be filled with the Holy Spirit; join a church where the members believe the Bible and know the Lord; seek the fellowship of other Christians; learn and be nourished by God's Word and His many promises. Conversion is not the end of your journey—it is only the beginning." The work of nourishing your faith can and should be joyful work. The hours that you invest in Bible study, prayer, meditation, and worship should be times of enrichment and celebration. And, as you continue to build your life upon a foundation of faith, you will discover that the journey toward spiritual maturity lasts a lifetime.

In the space below, write down your thoughts about the rewards of being a faithful Christian.

_____

_____

_____

_____

_____

_____

## REAL REPENTANCE

*I preached to those in Damascus first, and to those in Jerusalem and in all the region of Judea, and to the Gentiles, that they should repent and turn to God, and do works worthy of repentance.*

Acts 26:20 HCSB

Who among us has sinned? All of us. But the good news is this: When we do ask God's forgiveness and turn our hearts to Him, He forgives us absolutely and completely. Genuine repentance requires more than simply offering God apologies for our misdeeds. Real repentance may start with feelings of sorrow and remorse, but it ends only when we turn away from the sin that has heretofore distanced us from our Creator. In truth, we offer our most meaningful apologies to God, not with our words, but with our actions.

In the space below, write down your thoughts about repentance.

_____

_____

_____

_____

_____

_____

## BE CONFIDENT

*I have told you these things so that in Me you may have peace. In the world you have suffering. But take courage! I have conquered the world.*

John 16:33 HCSB

As a Christian, you have many reasons to be confident. After all, God is in His heaven; Christ has risen; and you are the recipient of God's grace. Despite these blessings, you may, from time to time, find yourself being tormented by negative emotions—and you are certainly not alone.

Even the most faithful Christians are overcome by occasional bouts of fear and doubt. You are no different. But even when you feel very distant from God, remember that God is never distant from you. When you sincerely seek His presence, He will touch your heart, calm your fears, and restore your confidence.

In the space below, write down your thoughts about God's promises and what those promises mean to you.

_____

_____

_____

_____

_____

## GOOD THINKING

*Guard your heart above all else, for it is the source of life.*

Proverbs 4:23 HCSB

Are you a person whose hopes and dreams are alive and well? Do you regularly put a smile on your face? And then, do you share that smile with family and friends? Hopefully so. After all, when you decided to allow Christ to rule over your heart, you entitled yourself to share in His promise of spiritual abundance and eternal joy. But sometimes, when pessimism and doubt invade your thoughts, you won't feel like celebrating. Why? Because thoughts are intensely powerful things. Today, spend more time thinking about your blessings, and less time fretting about your hardships. Then, take time to thank the Giver of all things good for gifts that are, in truth, far too numerous to count.

In the space below, thank God for His blessings, His promises, and His Son.

_____

_____

_____

_____

_____

_____

## FAITH VERSUS FEAR

*Do not fear, for I am with you; do not be afraid, for I am your God. I will strengthen you; I will help you; I will hold on to you with My righteous right hand.*

Isaiah 41:10 HCSB

A terrible storm rose quickly on the Sea of Galilee, and the disciples were afraid. Although they had witnessed many miracles, the disciples feared for their lives, so they turned to Jesus, and He calmed the waters and the wind. The next time you find yourself facing a fear-provoking situation, remember that the One who calmed the wind and the waves is also your personal Savior. Then ask yourself which is stronger: your faith or your fear. The answer should be obvious. So, when the storm clouds form overhead, remember this: Wherever you are, God is there, too. And, because He cares for you, you are protected.

In the space below, write down your thoughts about God's love for you and your family.

_____

_____

_____

_____

_____

## BE PROACTIVE ABOUT
## YOUR HEALTH

*A prudent person foresees the danger ahead and takes precautions; the simpleton goes blindly on and suffers the consequences.*

Proverbs 22:3 NLT

You're the human being whom God has entrusted with the responsibility of caring for your body. And of this you can be sure: it's always the right time to become proactive about your health. Eating unhealthy foods is habit-forming. And if you have acquired the unfortunate habit of eating unhealthy foods, then God wants you start making changes today.

In the space below, write down at least three healthy choices you need to make today.

_____

_____

_____

_____

_____

_____

## SPIRITUAL RENEWAL

*Therefore if anyone is in Christ, he is a new creature; the old things passed away; behold, new things have come.*

2 Corinthians 5:17 HCSB

Even the most inspired Christians may, from time to time, find themselves running on empty. The demands of daily life can drain us of our strength and rob us of the joy that is rightfully ours in Christ. Are you tired or troubled? Turn your heart toward God in prayer. Are you weak or worried? Take the time—or, more accurately, make the time—to delve deeply into God's Holy Word. Are you spiritually depleted? Call upon fellow believers to support you, and call upon Christ to renew your spirit and your life. When you do, you'll discover that the Creator of the universe stands always ready and always able to create a new sense of wonderment and joy in you.

In the space below, write down your thoughts about God's ability to renew your strength.

## THE SIMPLE LIFE

*Whoever becomes simple and elemental again, like this child,
will rank high in God's kingdom.*

Matthew 18:4 MSG

---

You live in a world where simplicity is in short supply.
Think for a moment about the complexity of your everyday life and compare it to the lives of your ancestors.
Certainly, you are the beneficiary of many technological
innovations, but those innovations have a price: in all
likelihood, your world is highly complex. Unless you take
firm control of your time and your life, you may be overwhelmed by an ever-increasing tidal wave of complexity
that threatens your happiness. But God understands the
joy of living simply, and so should you. So do yourself a
favor: keep your life as simple as possible. By simplifying
your life, you are destined to improve it.

---

In the space below, write down your thoughts about the
advantages of simplicity.

---

---

---

---

---

# THE POWER OF PRAYER

*The intense prayer of the righteous is very powerful.*

James 5:16 HCSB

The quality of your spiritual life will be in direct proportion to the quality of your prayer life. Prayer changes things, and it changes you. Today, instead of turning things over in your mind, turn them over to God in prayer. Instead of worrying about your next decision, ask God to lead the way. Pray constantly about things great and small. God is listening, and He wants to hear from you now.

In the space below, make a list of things you need to pray about today.

_____

_____

_____

_____

_____

_____

_____

_____

_____

# PRAISE HIM

*Give thanks to the Lord, for He is good; His faithful love endures forever.*

Psalm 106:1 HCSB

Sometimes, in our rush "to get things done," we simply don't stop long enough to pause and thank our Creator for the countless blessings He has bestowed upon us. But when we slow down and express our gratitude to the One who made us, we enrich our own lives and the lives of those around us. Thanksgiving should become a habit, a regular part of our daily routines. God has blessed us beyond measure, and we owe Him everything, including our eternal praise. Let us praise Him today, tomorrow, and throughout eternity.

In the space below, praise God for His blessings, for His Word, and for His Son.

_____

_____

_____

_____

_____

_____

_____

# YOUR BODY IS A GIFT

*Do you not know that you are the temple of God and that the Spirit of God dwells in you?*

1 Corinthians 3:16 NKJV

As you petition God each morning, ask Him for the strength and the wisdom to treat your body as His creation and His "temple." During the day ahead, you will face countless temptations to do otherwise, but with God's help, you can treat your body as the priceless, one-of-a-kind gift that it most certainly is.

In the space below, make a promise to God that you will care for the body He has given you.

_____

_____

_____

_____

_____

_____

_____

_____

_____

## TRUST THE SHEPHERD

*The Lord is my shepherd; I shall not want. He makes me to lie down in green pastures; He leads me beside the still waters. He restores my soul.*

Psalm 23:1-3 NKJV

In the 23rd Psalm, David teaches us that God is like a watchful shepherd caring for his flock. No wonder these verses have provided comfort and hope for generations of believers. On occasion, you will confront circumstances that trouble you to the very core of your soul. When you are afraid, trust in God. When you are worried, turn your concerns over to Him. When you are anxious, be still and listen for the quiet assurance of God's promises. And then, place your life in His hands. He is your Shepherd today and throughout eternity. Trust the Shepherd.

In the space below, thank the Shepherd for His guidance and protection.

_____

_____

_____

_____

_____

_____

# YOUR BODY, YOUR RESPONSIBILITY

*So then each of us shall give account of himself to God.*

Romans 14:12 NKJV

When our unhealthy habits lead to poor health, we find it all too easy to look beyond ourselves and assign blame. In fact, we live in a society where blame has become a national obsession: we blame cigarette manufacturers, restaurants, and food producers, to name only a few. But to blame others is to miss the point: We, and we alone, are responsible for the way that we treat our bodies. And the sooner that we accept that responsibility, the sooner we can assert control over our bodies and our lives.

In the space below, write down your thoughts about the futility of blaming others for decisions you've made.

_____

_____

_____

_____

_____

_____

_____

_____

# HEALTHY FOODS AND WISE CHOICES

*I have set before you life and death, blessings and curses. Now choose life, so that you and your children may live and that you may love the LORD your God, listen to his voice, and hold fast to him.*

Deuteronomy 30:19-20 NIV

But for those of us who have become accustomed to large quantities of full-flavored, high-calorie foods, old memories indeed die hard. Should we count every calorie that we ingest from now until the day the Good Lord calls us home? Probably not. When we focus too intently upon weight reduction, we may make weight loss even harder to achieve. Instead, we should eliminate from our diets the foods that are obviously bad for us and we should eat more of the foods that are obviously good for us. And of course, we should eat sensible amounts, not prodigious portions.

In the space below, make a list of any unhealthy foods that you should eliminate from your diet.

_____

_____

_____

_____

_____

## OUR FEAR-BASED WORLD

*They do not fear bad news; they confidently trust the Lord to care for them. They are confident and fearless and can face their foes triumphantly.*

Psalm 112:7-8 NLT

We live in a fear-based world, a world where bad news travels at light speed and good news doesn't. These are troubled times, times when we have legitimate fears for the future of our nation, our world, and our families. But as Christians, we have every reason to live courageously. After all, the ultimate battle has already been fought and won on that faraway cross at Calvary. Your Heavenly Father is your Protector and your Deliverer. Call upon Him in your hour of need, and be comforted. Whatever your challenge, whatever your trouble, God can handle it.

In the space below, write down your thoughts about God's ability to handle your challenges.

_____

_____

_____

_____

_____

_____

## FEARING GOD

*The fear of the Lord is the beginning of knowledge.*

Proverbs 1:7 HCSB

Are you a person who possesses a healthy, fearful respect for God's power? Hopefully so. After all, God's Word teaches that the fear of the Lord is the beginning of knowledge. When we fear the Creator—and when we honor Him by obeying His commandments—we receive God's approval and His blessings. But, when we ignore Him or disobey His commandments, we invite disastrous consequences. So today, as you face the realities of everyday life, remember this: until you acquire a healthy, respectful fear of God's power, your education is incomplete, and so is your faith.

In the space below, write down your thoughts about the dangers of displeasing God.

_____

_____

_____

_____

_____

_____

_____

_____

## IN THE FOOTSTEPS OF THE SAVIOR

*The one who loves his life will lose it, and the one who hates his life in this world will keep it for eternal life. If anyone serves Me, he must follow Me. Where I am, there My servant also will be. If anyone serves Me, the Father will honor him.*

John 12:25-26 HCSB

Whom will you walk with today? Will you walk with people who worship the ways of the world? Or will you walk with the Son of God? Jesus walks with you. Are you walking with Him? Hopefully, you will choose to walk with Him today and every day of your life. Charles Stanley advised, "A disciple is a follower of Christ. That means you take on His priorities as your own. His agenda becomes your agenda. His mission becomes your mission." Jesus made incredible sacrifices for mankind and for you. What sacrifices will you make today for Him?

In the space below, write down your thoughts about Christ's love.

_____

_____

_____

_____

_____

_____

## YOUR WAY OR GOD'S WAY

*A man's heart plans his way, but the Lord determines his steps.*

Proverbs 16:9 HCSB

The popular song "My Way" is a perfectly good tune, but it's not a perfect guide for life. If you're looking for life's perfect prescription, you'd better forget about doing things your way and start doing things God's way. The most important decision of your life is, of course, your commitment to accept Jesus Christ as your personal Lord and Savior. And once your eternal destiny is secured, you will undoubtedly ask yourself the question "What now, Lord?" Sometimes, God's plans are crystal clear; sometimes they are not. So be patient, keep searching, and keep praying. At the proper time, God will answer your prayers and make His plans known. You'll discover those plans by doing things His way . . . and you'll be eternally grateful that you did.

In the space below, write down a few of your thoughts about God's plan for your life.

_____

_____

_____

_____

_____

# KEEP LEARNING HOW TO STAY FIT

*The wise store up knowledge, but the mouth of the fool hastens destruction.*

Proverbs 10:14 HCSB

You don't have to attend medical school to understand the basic principles of maintaining a healthy lifestyle. In fact, many of the things you need to know are contained in this text. But don't stop here. Vow to make yourself an expert on the care and feeding of the body that God has given you. In today's information-packed world, becoming an expert isn't a very hard thing to do.

In the space below, list several places where you can learn more about health and fitness.

_____

_____

_____

_____

_____

_____

_____

_____

## MENTORS THAT MATTER

*The lips of the righteous feed many.*

Proverbs 10:21 HCSB

Here's a simple yet effective way to strengthen your faith: Choose role models whose faith in God is strong. When you emulate godly people, you become a more godly person yourself. That's why you should seek out mentors who, by their words and their presence, make you a better person and a better Christian. Today, as a gift to yourself, select, from your friends and family members, a mentor whose judgment you trust. Then listen carefully to your mentor's advice and be willing to accept that advice, even if accepting it requires effort, or pain, or both.

In the space below, list several people whom you consider to be mentors.

_____

_____

_____

_____

_____

_____

_____

_____

## MISTAKES HAPPEN

*Have mercy on me, O God, according to your unfailing love;*
*according to your great compassion blot out my transgressions.*
*Wash away all my iniquity and cleanse me from my sin.*

Psalm 51:1-2 NIV

We are imperfect women living in an imperfect world; mistakes are simply part of the price we pay for being here. But, even though mistakes are an inevitable part of life's journey, repeated mistakes should not be. When we commit the inevitable blunders of life, we must correct them, learn from them, and pray to God for the wisdom not to repeat them. And then, if we are successful, our mistakes become lessons, and our lives become adventures in growth, not stagnation.

In the space below, write down a mistake you made that taught you a valuable lesson.

_____

_____

_____

_____

_____

_____

# NEW BEGINNINGS

*I will give you a new heart and put a new spirit within you.*

Ezekiel 36:26 HCSB

---

If we sincerely want to change ourselves for the better, we must start on the inside and work our way out from there. Lasting change doesn't occur "out there"; it occurs "in here." It occurs, not in the shifting sands of our own particular circumstances, but in the quiet depths of our own hearts.

Are you in search of a new beginning or, for that matter, a new you? If so, don't expect changing circumstances to miraculously transform you into the person you want to become. Transformation starts with God, and it starts in the silent center of a humble human heart—like yours.

---

In the space below, write down your thoughts about God's ability to renew your spirit.

_____

_____

_____

_____

_____

_____

_____

## THE WISDOM TO OBEY

*And the world with its lust is passing away, but the one who does God's will remains forever.*

1 John 2:17 HCSB

---

It's simple: When you're treating your body like a temple, you're obeying God; when you're abusing your body, you're disobeying Him. And make no mistake: disobedience is easy. Since God created Adam and Eve, we human beings have been rebelling against our Creator. Why? Because we are unwilling to trust God's Word, and we are unwilling to follow His commandments. Talking about God is easy; living by His commandments is considerably harder. But, unless we are willing to abide by God's laws, all of our righteous proclamations ring hollow. How can we best proclaim our love for the Lord? By obeying Him. And, for further instructions, read the manual.

---

In the space below, write down your thoughts about the dangers of disobeying God's commandments.

---

---

---

---

---

## GLORIOUS OPPORTUNITIES

*Make the most of every opportunity.*

Colossians 4:5 NIV

Are you excited about the opportunities of today and thrilled by the possibilities of tomorrow? Do you confidently expect God to lead you to a place of abundance, peace, and joy? If you trust God's promises, and if you have welcomed God's Son into your heart, then you believe that your future is intensely and eternally bright.

Today, as you prepare to meet the duties of everyday life, pause and consider God's promises. And then think for a moment about the wonderful future that awaits all believers, including you. God has promised that your future is secure. Trust that promise, and celebrate the life of abundance and eternal joy that is now yours through Christ.

In the space below, write down at least one opportunity you'll have today to improve your physical or spiritual health.

_____

_____

_____

_____

_____

## A PASSIONATE LIFE

*Never be lazy in your work, but serve the Lord enthusiastically.*

Romans 12:11 NLT

As a thoughtful Christian, you have every reason to be enthusiastic about life, but sometimes the inevitable struggles may cause you to feel decidedly unenthusiastic. If you feel that your enthusiasm is slowly fading away, it's time to slow down, to rest, to count your blessings, and to pray. When you feel worried or weary, you must pray fervently for God to renew your sense of wonderment and excitement. Life with God can be—and should be—a glorious adventure. Revel in it. When you do, God will most certainly smile upon your work and your life.

In the space below, write down several things you're passionate about.

_____

_____

_____

_____

_____

_____

_____

## YOU NEED ENDURANCE

*But endurance must do its complete work, so that you may be mature and complete, lacking nothing.*

James 1:4 HCSB

Physical fitness is not the result of a single decision that is made "once and for all." Physical fitness results from thousands of decisions that are made day after day, week after week, and year after year. The Bible teaches us to persevere: "For you need endurance, so that after you have done God's will, you may receive what was promised." These reassuring words from Hebrews 10:36 (HCSB) remind us that when we persevere, we will eventually receive that which God has promised.

In the space below, ask God to help you make wise choices today and every day.

_____

_____

_____

_____

_____

_____

_____

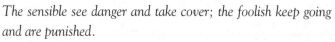

## SAFETY FIRST

*The sensible see danger and take cover; the foolish keep going and are punished.*

Proverbs 27:12 HCSB

---

Some risk takers are easy to spot: they jump out of airplanes, scurry up tall mountains, or race very fast automobiles. Most are not so bold; instead, they take more subtle risks: Drinking and driving, or smoking cigarettes, or neglecting their seatbelts, or any countless other behaviors that, while not as glamorous as skydiving, are equally as dangerous. This world holds enough hazards of its own without our adding to them by foolishly neglecting our own personal safety and the safety of others. The next time you're tempted to do something foolish, remember that the body you're putting at risk belongs not only to you, but also to God. Behave wisely.

---

In the space below, write down your thoughts on how you need to improve your safety.

_____

_____

_____

_____

_____

_____

## THE WORLD . . . AND YOU

*Don't copy the behavior and customs of this world, but let God transform you into a new person by changing the way you think.*

Romans 12:2 NLT

We live in the world, but we must not worship it. Our duty is to place God first and everything else second. But because we are fallible beings with imperfect faith, placing God in His rightful place is often difficult. In fact, at every turn, or so it seems, we are tempted to do otherwise. The 21st-century world is a noisy, distracting place filled with countless opportunities to stray from God's will. The world seems to cry, "Worship me with your time, your money, your energy, and your thoughts!" But God commands otherwise: He commands us to worship Him and Him alone; everything else must be secondary.

In the space below, write down your thoughts about the dangers of becoming too engrossed in the popular media.

_____

_____

_____

_____

_____

# DISTRUST THE MEDIA MESSAGES

*Do you not know that friendship with the world is hostility toward God? So whoever wants to be the world's friend becomes God's enemy.*

James 4:4 HCSB

Many of the messages that you receive from the media are specifically designed to sell you products that interfere with your spiritual, physical, or emotional health. God takes great interest in your health; the moguls from Madison Avenue take great interest in your pocketbook. Trust God.

In the space below, write down your thoughts about the dangers of becoming too friendly with the world.

_____

_____

_____

_____

_____

_____

_____

_____

## WHAT KIND OF EXAMPLE?

*Set an example of good works yourself, with integrity and dignity in your teaching.*

Titus 2:7 HCSB

---

What kind of example are you? Are you the kind of person whose life serves as a powerful example of decency and morality? If so, you are not only blessed by God, you are also a powerful force for good in a world that desperately needs positive influences such as yours. The sermons that we live are far more compelling than the ones we preach. So remember this: whether you like it or not, your life is an accurate reflection of your creed. If this fact gives you cause for concern, don't bother talking about the changes that you intend to make—make them. And then, when your good deeds speak for themselves—as they most certainly will—don't interrupt.

---

In the space below, write down your thoughts about the importance of being a positive role model.

---

---

---

---

---

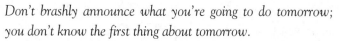

# IN HIS HANDS

*Don't brashly announce what you're going to do tomorrow;*
*you don't know the first thing about tomorrow.*

Proverbs 27:1 MSG

The old saying is both familiar and true: "Man proposes
and God disposes." Our world unfolds according to God's
plans, not our wishes. Thus, boasting about future events
is to be avoided by those who acknowledge God's sover-
eignty over all things.

Are you planning for a better tomorrow for yourself
and your family? If so, you are to be congratulated: God rewards forethought in the same way that He often punishes
impulsiveness. But as you make your plans, do so with
humility, with gratitude, and with trust in your Heavenly
Father. His hand directs the future; to think otherwise is
both arrogant and naïve.

In the space below, write down a few important goals concerning your faith, your fitness, and your future.

_____

_____

_____

_____

_____

## ABUNDANT PEACE

*And the peace of God, which surpasses every thought, will guard your hearts and your minds in Christ Jesus.*

Philippians 4:7 HCSB

Are you the kind of person who accepts God's spiritual abundance without reservation? If so, you are availing yourself of the peace and the joy that He has promised. Do you sincerely seek the riches that our Savior offers to those who give themselves to Him? Then follow Him. When you do, you will receive the love and the abundance that Jesus offers to those who follow Him.

In the space below, write down your thoughts about the earthly joys and heavenly rewards of following Jesus.

_____

_____

_____

_____

_____

_____

_____

_____

## A HELPING HAND

*The greatest among you will be your servant. Whoever exalts himself will be humbled, and whoever humbles himself will be exalted.*

Matthew 23:11-12 HCSB

Jesus has much to teach us about generosity. He teaches that the most esteemed men and women are not the self-congratulatory leaders of society but are, instead, the humblest of servants. If you were being graded on generosity, how would you score? Would you earn "A"s in philanthropy and humility? Hopefully so. But if your grades could stand a little improvement, this is the perfect day to begin. Today, you may feel the urge to hoard your blessings. Don't do it. Instead, give generously to your neighbors, and do so without fanfare. Find a need and fill it. Lend a helping hand and share a word of kindness. This is God's way.

In the space below, write down at least one person who needs your help today.

_____

_____

_____

_____

_____

# THE CORNERSTONE

*Let us fix our eyes on Jesus, the author and perfecter of our faith, who for the joy set before him endured the cross, scorning its shame, and sat down at the right hand of the throne of God.*

Hebrews 12:2 NIV

God has given you the gift of eternal life through His Son. In response to God's priceless gift, you are instructed to focus your thoughts, your prayers, and your energies upon God and His only begotten Son. To do so, you must resist the subtle yet powerful temptation to become a "spiritual dabbler." A person who dabbles in the Christian faith is unwilling to place God above all other things. Resist that temptation; make God the cornerstone and the touchstone of your life.

In the space below, write down what "focusing on Jesus" means to you.

_____

_____

_____

_____

_____

_____

_____

## GUARD YOUR HEART AND MIND

*Finally, brethren, whatever things are true, whatever things are noble, whatever things are just, whatever things are pure, whatever things are lovely, whatever things are of good report, if there is any virtue and if there is anything praiseworthy—meditate on these things.*

Philippians 4:8 NKJV

You are near and dear to God. He loves you more than you can imagine, and He wants the very best for you. And one more thing: God wants you to guard your heart. Every day, you are faced with choices . . . more choices than you can count. Today, the world will offer you countless opportunities to let down your guard and, by doing so, make needless mistakes that may injure you or your loved ones. So be watchful and obedient. Guard your heart by giving it to your Heavenly Father; it is safe with Him.

In the space below, write down a few things you can do to guard your heart from temptation and stress.

_____

_____

_____

_____

_____

_____

## RICHLY BLESSED

*The Lord bless you and keep you; the Lord make His face shine upon you, and be gracious to you.*

Numbers 6:24-25 NKJV

Because we have been so richly blessed, we should make thanksgiving a habit, a regular part of our daily routines. But sometimes, amid the stresses and obligations of everyday life, we may allow interruptions and distractions to interfere with the time we spend with God.

Have you counted your blessings today? And have you thanked God for them? Hopefully so. After all, God's gifts include your family, your friends, your talents, your opportunities, your possessions, and the priceless gift of eternal life. So today, as you go about the duties of everyday life, pause and give thanks to the Creator.

In the space below, write down some of the ways that God has blessed you and your loved ones.

_____

_____

_____

_____

_____

_____

## SAFE IN GOD'S HANDS

*When you pass through the waters, I will be with you; and through the rivers, they shall not overflow you. When you walk through the fire, you shall not be burned, nor shall the flame scorch you. For I am the Lord your God, The Holy One of Israel, your Savior.*

Isaiah 43:2-3 NKJV

Sometimes, in the crush of everyday life, God may seem far away, but He is not. God is everywhere you have ever been and everywhere you will ever go. He is with you night and day; He knows your thoughts and your prayers. He is your ultimate Protector. And, when you earnestly seek His protection, you will find it because He is here—always—waiting patiently for you to reach out to Him.

In the space below, jot down at least three times that God has protected you in the past.

_____

_____

_____

_____

_____

_____

_____

## GOD CAN HANDLE IT

*Your righteousness reaches heaven, God, You who have done great things; God, who is like You?*

Psalm 71:19 HCSB

It's a promise that is made over and over again in the Bible: Whatever "it" is, God can handle it. Are you running short on willpower? If so, perhaps you haven't yet asked God to give you strength. The Bible promises that God offers His power to those righteous men and women who earnestly seek it. If your willpower has failed you on numerous occasions, then it's time to turn your weaknesses over to God. If you've been having trouble standing on your own two feet, perhaps it's time to drop to your knees, in prayer.

In the space below, write down at least one healthy choice you can make today to improve your physical or spiritual health.

_____

_____

_____

_____

_____

_____

## MID-COURSE CORRECTIONS

*The sensible see danger and take cover; the foolish keep going and are punished.*

Proverbs 27:12 HCSB

In our fast-paced world, everyday life has become an exercise in managing change. Our circumstances change; our relationships change; our bodies change. We grow older every day, as does our world. Thankfully, God does not change. He is eternal, as are the truths that are found in His Holy Word. Are you facing one of life's inevitable "mid-course corrections"? If so, you must place your faith, your trust, and your life in the hands of the One who does not change: your Heavenly Father. He is the unmoving rock upon which you must construct this day and every day. When you do, you are secure.

In the space below, ask God to help you manage the changes that you are sure to face in the future.

_____

_____

_____

_____

_____

_____

## PATIENCE PAYS

*Rest in the Lord, and wait patiently for Him.*

Psalm 37:7 NKJV

For most of us, patience is a hard thing to master. Why? Because we have lots of things we want, and we know precisely when we want them: NOW (if not sooner). But our Father in heaven has other ideas; the Bible teaches that we must learn to wait patiently for the things that God has in store for us, even when waiting is difficult. Sometimes, patience is the price we pay for being responsible adults, and that's as it should be. After all, think about how patient our Heavenly Father has been with us.

In the space below, write down your thoughts about the rewards of being patient.

_____

_____

_____

_____

_____

_____

_____

## BEYOND GRUMPINESS

*The Lord bless you and keep you; the Lord make His face shine upon you, and be gracious to you.*

Numbers 6:24-25 NKJV

When the demands of life leave us rushing from place to place with scarcely a moment to spare, we may fail to pause and thank our Creator for His gifts. But, whenever we neglect to give proper thanks to the Father, we suffer because of our misplaced priorities. Christ promises us lives of abundance and joy if we accept His love and His grace. Yet sometimes, even the most righteous among us are beset by fits of ill temper and frustration. During these moments, we may not feel like turning our thoughts and prayers to Christ, but that's precisely what we should do. When we pray to Christ and acknowledge His gifts, we simply can't stay grumpy for long.

In the space below, thank God for His blessings.

_____

_____

_____

_____

_____

_____

## THE RIGHT KIND OF ATTITUDE

*May the words of my mouth and the meditation of my heart be acceptable to You, Lord, my rock and my Redeemer.*

Psalm 19:14 HCSB

What is your attitude today? Are you fearful or worried? Are you pessimistic about physical, emotional, or spiritual fitness? If so, it's time to have a little chat with your Father in heaven. God intends that your life be filled with spiritual abundance and joy—but God will not force His joy upon you—you must claim it for yourself. So do yourself this favor: accept God's gifts with a smile on your face, a song on your lips, and joy in your heart. Think optimistically about yourself and your future. Give thanks to the One who has given you everything, and trust in your heart that He wants to give you so much more.

Attitudes are contagious, so it's important to associate with people who are upbeat, optimistic, and encouraging. In the space below, make a short list of the people in your life who give you the most encouragement.

_____

_____

_____

_____

_____

## ENTHUSIASM FOR CHRIST

*Therefore, get your minds ready for action, being self-disciplined, and set your hope completely on the grace to be brought to you at the revelation of Jesus Christ. As obedient children, do not be conformed to the desires of your former ignorance but, as the One who called you is holy, you also are to be holy in all your conduct.*

1 Peter 1:13-15 HCSB

John Wesley advised, "Catch on fire with enthusiasm and people will come for miles to watch you burn." His words still ring true. When we fan the flames of enthusiasm for Christ, our faith serves as a beacon to others. Our world desperately needs faithful believers who share the Good News of Jesus with joyful exuberance. Be such a person. The world desperately needs your enthusiasm—and your testimony—now!

In the space below, jot down a few of the benefits you receive when you're enthusiastic.

_____

_____

_____

_____

_____

_____

## ENDURING DIFFICULT DAYS

*I have heard your prayer, I have seen your tears; surely I will heal you.*

2 Kings 20:5 NKJV

From time to time, all of us must endure discouragement. And, we sometimes experience life-changing personal losses that leave us reeling. When we do, God stands ready to protect us. When we are troubled, we must call upon God, and, in His own time and according to His own plan, He will heal us. Are you anxious about your faith or your fitness? Take those anxieties to God. Are you troubled? Take your troubles to Him. Does your world seem to be trembling beneath your feet? Seek protection from the One who cannot be moved. The same God who created the universe will protect you if you ask Him. So ask.

In the space below, write down at least three things you can do whenever your faith is tested.

_____

_____

_____

_____

_____

_____

## THE SERMON YOU LIVE

*Set an example of good works yourself, with integrity and dignity in your teaching.*

Titus 2:7 HCSB

Your life is a sermon. What kind of sermon will you preach today about your faith and your fitness? The words you choose to speak may have some impact on others, but not nearly as much impact as the life you choose to live. Today, pause to consider the tone, the theme, and the context of your particular sermon, and ask yourself if it's a message that you're proud to deliver.

In the space below, write your thoughts about the need to be a positive role model for your family and friends.

_____

_____

_____

_____

_____

_____

_____

_____

## ABUNDANT LIVING

*I came so they can have real and eternal life, more and better life than they ever dreamed of.*

John 10:10 MSG

God wants you to experience abundant life, but He will not force you to adopt a healthy lifestyle. Managing your food and your fitness is up to you. Christ is the ultimate Savior of mankind and the personal Savior of those who believe in Him. As His servants, we should place Him at the very center of our lives. And, every day that God gives us breath, we should share Christ's love and His abundance with a world that needs both.

In the space below, thank God for the spiritual abundance that is yours when you follow His Son.

_____

_____

_____

_____

_____

_____

_____

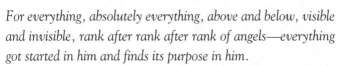

## DISCOVERING GOD'S PURPOSE FOR YOUR LIFE

*For everything, absolutely everything, above and below, visible and invisible, rank after rank after rank of angels—everything got started in him and finds its purpose in him.*

Colossians 1:16 MSG

Do you sincerely seek to discover God's purpose for your life? If so, you must first be willing to live in accordance with His commandments. You must also study God's Word and be watchful for His signs. You should open yourself up to the Creator every day—beginning with this one—and you must have faith that He will soon reveal His plans to you. And finally, since a healthy lifestyle is what God wants for you, isn't it what you should strive for, too?

In the space below, write down a few things that you believe God wants you to accomplish today.

_____

_____

_____

_____

_____

_____

_____

# THE NEW YOU

*If anyone belongs to Christ, there is a new creation. The old things have gone; everything is made new!*

2 Corinthians 5:17 NCV

Have you invited God's Son to reign over your heart and your life? If so, think for a moment about the "old" you, the person you were before you invited Christ into your heart. Now, think about the "new" you, the person you have become since then. Is there a difference between the "old" you and the "new and improved" version? There should be! And that difference should be noticeable not only to you but also to others.

In the space below, write down several things you do differently because you're a Christian.

_____

_____

_____

_____

_____

_____

_____

## TODAY'S LESSON

*Start with God—the first step in learning is bowing down to God.*

Proverbs 1:7 MSG

Today is your classroom: what will you learn? Will you use today's experiences as tools for personal, spiritual, and physical improvement, or will you ignore the lessons that life and God are trying to teach you? Will you carefully study God's Word, and will you apply His teachings to the experiences of everyday life? The events of today have much to teach. You have much to learn. May you live—and learn—accordingly.

In the space below, write down a lesson that you think God is trying to teach you today.

_____

_____

_____

_____

_____

_____

_____

_____

# TAKE RESPONSIBILITY FOR YOUR HEALTH

*So then each of us shall give account of himself to God.*

Romans 14:12 NKJV

If you want to establish a healthy lifestyle, you need to assume responsibility for your actions. Once you begin to hold yourself accountable, you'll begin to grow emotionally and spiritually. John Maxwell observed, "The key to healthy eating is moderation and managing what you eat every day." And he was right. Crash diets don't usually work, but sensible eating habits do work, so plan your meals accordingly.

Today, write down a few of the foods that you should probably eliminate from your diet.

_____

_____

_____

_____

_____

_____

_____

_____

## TO GOD BE THE GLORY

*Clothe yourselves with humility toward one another, because God resists the proud, but gives grace to the humble.*

1 Peter 5:5 HCSB

As Christians, we have a profound reason to be humble: We have been refashioned and saved by Jesus Christ, and that salvation came not because of our own good works but because of God's grace. Thus, we are not "self-made"; we are "God-made" and "Christ-saved." How, then, can we be boastful? Dietrich Bonhoeffer observed, "It is very easy to overestimate the importance of our own achievements in comparison with what we owe others." In other words, reality breeds humility. So, instead of puffing out your chest and saying, "Look at me!", give credit where credit is due, starting with God.

In the space below, write down your thoughts on the dangers of being too prideful.

_____

_____

_____

_____

_____

_____

## HOW TO TREAT OTHERS

*Therefore, whatever you want others to do for you, do also the same for them—this is the Law and the Prophets.*

Matthew 7:12 HCSB

---

Would you like to make the world a better place? If so, you can start by practicing the Golden Rule. Jesus made Himself perfectly clear: He instructed you to treat other people in the same way that you want to be treated. But sometimes, especially when you're feeling the pressures of everyday living, obeying the Golden Rule can seem like an impossible task—but it's not. So if you want to know how to treat other people, ask the person you see every time you look into the mirror. The answer you receive will tell you exactly what to do.

---

In the space below, write down your thoughts on the rewards of being kind.

---

---

---

---

---

---

---

## LIVING IN CHRIST'S LOVE

*So now, little children, remain in Him, so that when He appears we may have boldness and not be ashamed before Him at His coming.*

1 John 2:28-29 HCSB

Even though we are imperfect, fallible human beings, even though we have fallen far short of God's commandments, Christ loves us still. His love is perfect and steadfast; it does not waver—it does not change. Our task, as believers, is to accept Christ's love and to encourage others to do likewise. In today's troubled world, we all need the love and the peace that is found through the Son of God. Thankfully, Christ's love has no limits; it can encircle all of us. And it's up to each of us to ensure that it does.

In the space below, write down your thoughts about the sacrifice Christ made for you.

_____

_____

_____

_____

_____

_____

_____

# CONTENTMENT THROUGH CHRIST

*The LORD will give strength to His people; the LORD will bless His people with peace.*

Psalm 29:11 NKJV

Do you sincerely want to be a contented Christian? Then set your mind and your heart upon God's love and His grace. Seek first the salvation that is available through a personal relationship with Jesus Christ, and then claim the joy, the contentment, and the spiritual abundance that the Shepherd offers His sheep.

In the space below, write down a few of your thoughts about contentment.

_____

_____

_____

_____

_____

_____

_____

_____

_____

## DISCIPLINE WINS THE RACE

*Finishing is better than starting. Patience is better than pride.*

Ecclesiastes 7:8 NLT

A well-lived life is like a marathon, not a sprint—it calls for preparation, determination, and, of course, lots of discipline. It takes discipline to strengthen your faith, and it takes discipline to improve your fitness. So, the next time you come face-to-face with a tough challenge, don't back down and don't worry. Just do the work in front of you today, and leave the rest up to God.

Today, write down your ideas about the costs and the benefits of self-discipline.

_____

_____

_____

_____

_____

_____

_____

_____

_____

## ABOVE AND BEYOND OUR CIRCUMSTANCES

*Should we accept only good from God and not adversity?*

Job 2:10 HCSB

All of us face difficult days. Sometimes even the most devout Christian can become discouraged, and you are no exception. After all, you live in a world where expectations can be high and demands can be even higher. If you find yourself enduring difficult circumstances, remember that God remains in His heaven. If you become discouraged with the direction of your day or your life, turn your thoughts and prayers to Him. He is a God of possibility, not negativity. He will guide you through your difficulties and beyond them . . . far beyond.

In the space below, write down your thoughts about what it takes to overcome tough times.

_____

_____

_____

_____

_____

_____

_____

# THE POWER OF OUR WORDS

*No rotten talk should come from your mouth, but only what is good for the building up of someone in need, in order to give grace to those who hear.*

Ephesians 4:29 HCSB

The words that we speak have the power to do great good or great harm. If we speak words of encouragement and hope, we can lift others up. And that's exactly what God commands us to do! Sometimes, when we feel uplifted and secure, it is easy to speak kind words. Other times, when we are discouraged or tired, we can scarcely summon the energy to uplift ourselves, much less anyone else. God intends that we speak words of kindness, wisdom, and truth, no matter our circumstances, no matter our emotions. When we do, we share a priceless gift with the world, and we give glory to the One who gave His life for us. As believers, we must do no less.

In the space below, write down the names of at least three people who need your encouragement today.

_____

_____

_____

_____

_____

## A POSITIVE INFLUENCE

*Be an example to the believers in word, in conduct, in love, in spirit, in faith, in purity.*

1 Timothy 4:12 NKJV

As followers of Christ, we must each ask ourselves an important question: "What kind of example am I?" The answer to that question determines, in large part, whether or not we are positive influences on our own little corners of the world. Are you the kind of Christian whose actions, day in and day out, are based upon integrity, fidelity, and a love for the Lord? If so, you are not only blessed by God, you are also a powerful force for good in a world that desperately needs positive influences such as yours.

In the space below, write down your thoughts about the need to be a good example.

_____

_____

_____

_____

_____

_____

## HIS GENEROSITY . . . AND YOURS

*But God proves His own love for us in that while we were still sinners Christ died for us!*

Romans 5:8 HCSB

Christ showed His love for us by willingly sacrificing His own life so that we might have eternal life. We, as Christ's followers, are challenged to share His love. And, when we walk each day with Jesus—and obey the commandments found in God's Holy Word—we are worthy ambassadors for Him. Just as Christ has been—and will always be—the ultimate friend to His flock, so should we be Christ-like in our love and generosity to those in need. When we share the love of Christ, we share a priceless gift. As His servants, we must do no less.

In the space below, write down the names of at least three people who need your kindness today.

_____

_____

_____

_____

_____

_____

## HIS RIGHTFUL PLACE

*You shall have no other gods before Me.*

Exodus 20:3 NKJV

When Jesus was tempted by Satan, the Master's response was unambiguous. Jesus chose to worship the Lord and serve Him only. We, as followers of Christ, must follow in His footsteps by placing God first. When we place God in a position of secondary importance, we do ourselves great harm. When we allow temptations or distractions to come between us and our Creator, we suffer. But, when we imitate Jesus and place the Lord in His rightful place—at the center of our lives—then we claim spiritual treasures that will endure forever.

In the space below, write down your thoughts about putting God first.

_____

_____

_____

_____

_____

_____

_____

## HIS COMFORTING HAND

*But God, who comforts the humble, comforted us . . . .*

2 Corinthians 7:6 HCSB

If you have been touched by the transforming hand of Jesus, then you have every reason to live courageously. Still, even if you are a dedicated Christian, you may find yourself discouraged by the inevitable disappointments and tragedies that occur in the lives of believers and non-believers alike. The next time you find your courage tested to the limit, lean upon God's promises. Trust His Son. When you are worried, anxious, or afraid, call upon your Creator and accept the touch of His comforting hand. Remember that God rules both mountaintops and valleys—with limitless wisdom and love—now and forever.

In the space below, write down your thoughts about God's love for you and your family.

_____

_____

_____

_____

_____

_____

# THE GIFT OF GRACE

*For by grace you are saved through faith, and this is not from yourselves; it is God's gift—not from works, so that no one can boast.*

Ephesians 2:8-9 HCSB

God has given us so many gifts, but none can compare with the gift of salvation. We have not earned our salvation; it is a gift from God. When we accept Christ into our hearts, we are saved by His grace. God's grace is the ultimate gift, and we owe to Him the ultimate in thanksgiving. Let us praise the Creator for His priceless gift, and let us share the Good News with all who cross our paths. We return our Father's love by accepting His grace and by sharing His message and His love. When we do, we are eternally blessed . . . and the Father smiles.

In the space below, write down your thoughts about God's priceless gift: the gift of eternal life.

_____

_____

_____

_____

_____

_____

## HIS INTIMATE LOVE

*As the Father loved Me, I also have loved you; abide in My love.*

John 15:9 NKJV

St. Augustine observed, "God loves each of us as if there were only one of us." Do you believe those words? Do you seek an intimate, one-on-one relationship with your Heavenly Father, or are you satisfied to keep Him at a "safe" distance? Sometimes, in the crush of your daily duties, God may seem far away, but He is not. God is everywhere you have ever been and everywhere you will ever go. He knows your thoughts and your prayers. And, when you earnestly seek Him, you will find Him because He is not far away. In fact He is right here, right now, always willing to talk. So what are you waiting for?

Today, jot down at least one important idea about God's plans for your spiritual or physical health.

_____

_____

_____

_____

_____

_____

## HIS HEALING TOUCH

*I am the Lord that healeth thee.*

Exodus 15:26 KJV

Are you concerned about your spiritual, physical, or emotional health? If so, there is a timeless source of comfort and assurance that is as near as your bookshelf. That source is the Holy Bible. God's Word has much to say about every aspect of your life, including your health. And, when you face concerns of any sort—including health-related challenges—God is with you. So trust your medical doctor to do his or her part, but place your ultimate trust in your benevolent Heavenly Father. His healing touch, like His love, endures forever.

In the space below, write down your thoughts about God's healing touch.

_____

_____

_____

_____

_____

_____

## TRUSTING HIS TIMING

*He told them, "You don't get to know the time. Timing is the Father's business."*

Acts 1:7 MSG

If you sincerely seek to be a person of faith, then you must learn to trust God's timing. You will be sorely tempted, however, to do otherwise. Because you are a fallible human being, you are impatient for things to happen. But, God knows better. God has created a world that unfolds according to His own timetable, not ours . . . thank goodness! We mortals might make a terrible mess of things. God does not. God's plan does not always happen in the way that we would like or at the time of our own choosing. Our task—as believing Christians who trust in a benevolent, all-knowing Father—is to wait patiently for God to reveal Himself. And reveal Himself He will.

In the space below, write down your thoughts about God's timing.

_____

_____

_____

_____

_____

## NEIGHBORS IN NEED

*Each one of us needs to look after the good of the people around us, asking ourselves, "How can I help?" That's exactly what Jesus did.*

Romans 15:2-3 MSG

Neighbors. We know that we are instructed to love them, and yet there's so little time...and we're so busy. No matter. As Christians, we are commanded by our Lord and Savior Jesus Christ to love our neighbors just as we love ourselves. Period. This very day, you will encounter someone who needs a word of encouragement, or a pat on the back, or a helping hand, or a heartfelt prayer. And, if you don't reach out to your friend, who will? If you don't take the time to understand the needs of your neighbors, who will? If you don't love your brothers and sisters, who will? So, today, look for a neighbor in need...and then do something to help. Father's orders.

In the space below, write down the names of at least five people you'll pray for throughout the day.

# FILLED WITH THE SPIRIT

*And don't get drunk with wine, which leads to reckless actions,*
*but be filled with the Spirit.*

Ephesians 5:18 HCSB

When you are filled with the Holy Spirit, your words and deeds will reflect a love and devotion to Christ. When you are filled with the Holy Spirit, the steps of your life's journey are guided by the Lord. When you allow God's Spirit to work in you and through you, you will be energized and transformed. Today, allow yourself to be filled with the Spirit of God. And then stand back in amazement as God begins to work miracles in your own life and in the lives of those you love.

In the space below, ask God to help you find the strength and discipline to meet your goals.

_____

_____

_____

_____

_____

_____

_____

## DISCOVERING HOPE

*These things I have spoken to you, that in Me you may have peace. In the world you will have tribulation; but be of good cheer, I have overcome the world.*

John 16:33 NKJV

There are few sadder sights on earth than the sight of a person who has lost all hope. In difficult times, hope can be elusive, but Christians need never lose it. After all, God is good; His love endures; He has promised His children the gift of eternal life. If you find yourself falling into the spiritual traps of worry and discouragement, consider the words of Jesus. It was Christ who promised, "In the world you will have tribulation; but be of good cheer, I have overcome the world." This world is indeed a place of trials and tribulations, but as believers, we are secure. God has promised us peace, joy, and eternal life. And, of course, God always keeps His promises.

In the space below, write down a few important goals concerning your faith, your fitness, and your future.

_____

_____

_____

_____

_____

## THE WISDOM TO BE HUMBLE

*Do nothing out of rivalry or conceit, but in humility consider others as more important than yourselves.*

Philippians 2:3 HCSB

God's Word clearly instructs us to be humble. And that's good because, as fallible human beings, we have so very much to be humble about! Yet some of us continue to puff ourselves up, seeming to say, "Look at me!" To do so is wrong. As Christians, we have been refashioned and saved by Jesus Christ, and that salvation came not because of our own good works but because of God's grace. How, then, can we be prideful? The answer, of course, is that, if we are honest with ourselves and with our God, we simply can't be boastful...we must, instead, be eternally grateful and exceedingly humble.

In the space below, write down your thoughts about the need to remain humble.

_____

_____

_____

_____

_____

_____

## KNOWLEDGE AND WISDOM

*A house is built by wisdom, and it is established by understanding; by knowledge the rooms are filled with every precious and beautiful treasure.*

Proverbs 24:3-4 HCSB

If we are to grow as Christians and as women, we need both knowledge and wisdom. Knowledge is found in textbooks. Wisdom, on the other hand, is found in God's Holy Word and in the carefully-chosen words of loving parents, family members, and friends. Knowledge is an important building block in a well-lived life, and it pays rich dividends both personally and professionally. But, wisdom is even more important because it refashions not only the mind, but also the heart.

Today, ask God to help you form healthier habits.

## SHARING THE GOOD NEWS

*As you go, announce this: "The kingdom of heaven has come near."*

Matthew 10:7 HCSB

The Good News of Jesus Christ should be shouted from the rooftops by believers the world over. But all too often, it is not. For a variety of reasons, many Christians keep their beliefs to themselves, and when they do, the world suffers because of their failure to speak up. As believers, we are called to share the transforming message of Jesus with our families, with our neighbors, and with the world. Jesus commands us to become fishers of men. And, the time to go fishing is now. We must share the Good News of Jesus Christ today—tomorrow may indeed be too late.

In the space below, write down the names of at least three people who need to hear about Jesus from you.

_____

_____

_____

_____

_____

## ON A MISSION

*But you are a chosen race, a royal priesthood, a holy nation, a people for His possession, so that you may proclaim the praises of the One who called you out of darkness into His marvelous light.*

1 Peter 2:9 HCSB

Whether you realize it or not, you are on a personal mission for God. As a Christian, that mission is straightforward: Honor God, accept Christ as your personal Savior, and serve God's children.

You will encounter these overriding purposes again and again as you worship your Creator and study His Word. Every day offers countless opportunities to serve God and to worship Him. When you do so, He will bless you in miraculous ways.

In the space below, jot down a few of your most important lifetime goals.

_____

_____

_____

_____

_____

_____

## SO MANY TEMPTATIONS

*No temptation has overtaken you except what is common to humanity. God is faithful and He will not allow you to be tempted beyond what you are able, but with the temptation He will also provide a way of escape, so that you are able to bear it.*

1 Corinthians 10:13 HCSB

This world is filled to the brim with temptations. Some of these temptations are small; eating a second scoop of ice cream, for example, is tempting, but not very dangerous. Other temptations, however, are not nearly so harmless. The devil is working 24/7, and he's causing pain and heartache in more ways than ever before. Thankfully, God is always with us, and He gives us the power to resist temptation whenever we ask Him for the strength to do so.

If you're not determined to be the master of your body, then you might just become a slave to your impulses. In the space below, write down your thoughts about God's ability to lead you from temptation.

_____

_____

_____

_____

_____

## NEVER-ENDING LOVE

*And we have this command from Him: the one who loves God must also love his brother.*

1 John 4:21 HCSB

C. S. Lewis observed, "A man's spiritual health is exactly proportional to his love for God." If we are to enjoy the spiritual health that God intends for us, we must praise Him, we must love Him, and we must obey Him.

When we worship God faithfully and obediently, we invite His love into our hearts. When we truly worship God, we allow Him to rule over our days and our lives. In turn, we grow to love God even more deeply as we sense His love for us. Today, open your heart to the Father. And let your obedience be a fitting response to His never-ending love.

Today, pick out one important obligation that you've been putting off. Then, take at least one specific step toward the completion of the task you've been avoiding.

_____

_____

_____

_____

_____

## CONFIDENT CHRISTIANITY

*You are my hope; O Lord GOD, You are my confidence.*

Psalm 71:5 NASB

We Christians have many reasons to be confident. God is in His heaven; Christ has risen, and we are the sheep of His flock. Yet sometimes, even the most devout Christians can become discouraged. Discouragement, however, is not God's way; He is a God of possibility not negativity. Are you a confident Christian? You should be. God's grace is eternal and His promises are unambiguous. So count your blessings, not your hardships. And live courageously. God is the Giver of all things good, and He watches over you today and forever.

In the space below, write down a few thoughts about your health and your future.

_____

_____

_____

_____

_____

_____

_____

## THY WILL BE DONE

*"Father, if it is Your will, take this cup away from Me; nevertheless not My will, but Yours, be done."*

Luke 22:42 NKJV

Before His crucifixion, Jesus went to the Mount of Olives and poured out His heart to God. Jesus knew of the agony that He was destined to endure, but He also knew that God's will must be done. We, like our Savior, face trials that bring fear and trembling to the very depths of our souls, but like Christ, we, too, must ultimately seek God's will, not our own. When we entrust our lives to Him completely and without reservation, He gives us the strength to meet any challenge, the courage to face any trial, and the wisdom to live in His righteousness.

In the space below, write down a few thoughts about the role that faith plays in your life.

_____

_____

_____

_____

_____

_____

_____

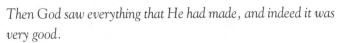

# HIS AWESOME CREATION

*Then God saw everything that He had made, and indeed it was very good.*

Genesis 1:31 NKJV

When we consider God's glorious universe, we marvel at the miracle of nature. The smallest seedlings and grandest stars are all part of God's infinite creation. God has placed His handiwork on display for all to see, and if we are wise, we will make time each day to celebrate the world that surrounds us.

Today, as you fulfill the demands of everyday life, pause to consider the majesty of heaven and earth. It is as miraculous as it is beautiful, as incomprehensible as it is breathtaking.

In the space below, praise God for His awesome creation.

_____

_____

_____

_____

_____

_____

_____

_____

## USING YOUR GIFTS

*I remind you to keep ablaze the gift of God that is in you.*

2 Timothy 1:6 HCSB

All people possess special gifts and talents; you are no exception. But, your gift is no guarantee of success; it must be cultivated and nurtured; otherwise, it will go unused…and God's gift to you will be squandered. Today, accept this challenge: value the talent that God has given you, nourish it, make it grow, and share it with the world. After all, the best way to say "Thank You" for God's gift is to use it.

In the space below, thank God for your gifts, and write down at least one specific thing you intend to do today to use your gifts.

_____

_____

_____

_____

_____

_____

_____

_____

_____

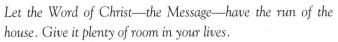

## GOD AND FAMILY

*Let the Word of Christ—the Message—have the run of the house. Give it plenty of room in your lives.*

Colossians 3:16 MSG

These are difficult days for our nation and for our families. But, thankfully, God is bigger than all of our challenges. God loves us and protects us. In times of trouble, He comforts us; in times of sorrow, He dries our tears. When we are troubled, or weak, or sorrowful, God is as near as our next breath.

Are you concerned for the well-being of your family? You are not alone. We live in a world where temptation and danger seem to lurk on every street corner. Parents and children alike have good reason to be watchful. But, despite the evils of our time, God remains steadfast. Even in these difficult days, no problem is too big for God.

In the space below, thank God for your family.

_____

_____

_____

_____

_____

_____

## PRIORITIES ... MOMENT BY MOMENT

*You can't go wrong when you love others. When you add up everything in the law code, the sum total is love. But make sure that you don't get so absorbed and exhausted in taking care of all your day-by-day obligations that you lose track of the time and doze off, oblivious to God.*

Romans 13:10-11 MSG

Each waking moment holds the potential to think a creative thought or offer a heartfelt prayer. God has filled this day with countless opportunities to love, to serve, and to seek His guidance. Seize those opportunities. And as a gift to yourself, to your family, and to the world, slow down and claim the inner peace that is your spiritual birthright: the peace of Jesus Christ.

In the space below, thank God for the gift of life and for the opportunity to exercise.

_____

_____

_____

_____

_____

_____

_____

## CELEBRATION WITH A SMILE

*Jacob said, "For what a relief it is to see your friendly smile. It is like seeing the smile of God!"*

Genesis 33:10 NLT

Life should never be taken for granted. Each day is a priceless gift from God and should be treated as such.

Hannah Whitall Smith observed, "How changed our lives would be if we could only fly through the days on wings of surrender and trust!" How true! Today, let us celebrate life with smiles on our faces and kind words on our lips. After all, this is God's day, and He has given us clear instructions for its use. We are commanded to rejoice and be glad. So, with no further ado, let the celebration begin.

In the space below, write down at least three things you intend to celebrate today.

_____

_____

_____

_____

_____

_____

_____

## THE GREATEST OF THESE

*Now these three remain: faith, hope, and love. But the greatest of these is love.*

1 Corinthians 13:13 HCSB

The beautiful words of 1st Corinthians 13 remind us that love is God's commandment: Faith is important, of course. So, too, is hope. But, love is more important still. We are commanded (not advised, not encouraged…commanded!) to love one another just as Christ loved us (John 13:34). That's a tall order, but as Christians, we are obligated to follow it. Christ showed His love for us on the cross, and we are called upon to return Christ's love by sharing it.

Today, be quiet and still. Then, in the silence, write down at least one person whom God is asking you to help.

_____

_____

_____

_____

_____

_____

_____

_____

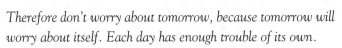

## COURAGE DURING TIMES
## OF CHANGE

*Therefore don't worry about tomorrow, because tomorrow will
worry about itself. Each day has enough trouble of its own.*

Matthew 6:34 HCSB

Are you anxious about situations that you cannot control? Take your anxieties to God. Are you troubled about changes that threaten to disrupt your life? Take your troubles to Him. Does your corner of the world seem to be trembling beneath your feet? Seek protection from the One who cannot be moved. The same God who created the universe will protect you if you ask Him . . . so ask Him . . . and then serve Him with willing hands and a trusting heart. And rest assured that the world may change moment by moment, but God's love endures—unfathomable and unchanging—forever.

In the space below, write down your thoughts about overcoming temporary setbacks.

_____

_____

_____

_____

_____

## A PATTERN OF GOOD WORKS

*In all things showing yourself to be a pattern of good works; in doctrine showing integrity, reverence, incorruptibility . . . .*

Titus 2:7 NKJV

Beth Moore correctly observed, "Those who walk in truth walk in liberty." And she was right. If you sincerely wish to walk "in liberty" with God, you must seek, to the best of your ability, to follow His commandments as you create a pattern of good works here on earth. When you do, the Father will bless you and keep you, now and forever.

In the space below, ask God to guide your steps today, tomorrow, and every day of your life.

_____

_____

_____

_____

_____

_____

_____

_____

_____

# HIS LOVE CHANGES EVERYTHING

*Your old life is dead. Your new life, which is your real life—even though invisible to spectators—is with Christ in God. He is your life.*

Colossians 3:3 MSG

Christ's love changes everything. His love is perfect and steadfast. Even though we are fallible and wayward, the Good Shepherd cares for us still. Even though we have fallen far short of the Father's commandments, Christ loves us with a power and depth that is beyond our understanding. And, as we accept Christ's love and walk in Christ's footsteps, our lives bear testimony to His power and to His grace. Yes, Christ's love changes everything; may we invite Him into our hearts so it can then change everything in us.

Today, jot down at least one thing you can do today to improve your spiritual or physical health.

_____

_____

_____

_____

_____

_____

## BEYOND THE DIFFICULTIES

*When you are in distress and all these things have happened to you, you will return to the Lord your God in later days and obey Him. He will not leave you, destroy you, or forget the covenant with your fathers that He swore to them by oath, because the Lord your God is a compassionate God.*

Deuteronomy 4:30-31 HCSB

Sometimes the traffic jams, and sometimes the dog gobbles the homework. But, when we find ourselves overtaken by the minor frustrations of life, we must catch ourselves, take a deep breath, and lift our thoughts upward. Although we are here on earth struggling to rise above the distractions of the day, we need never struggle alone. God is here—eternally and faithfully, with infinite patience and love—and, if we reach out to Him, He will restore perspective and peace to our souls.

In the space below, write down the most important problem that you need to solve today.

_____

_____

_____

_____

_____

# KEEP MAKING HEALTHY CHOICES

*I shall yet praise him, who is the health of my countenance, and my God.*

Psalm 42:11 KJV

God's plan for you includes provisions for your spiritual, physical, and emotional health. But, He expects you to do your fair share of the work! In a world that is chock-full of tasty temptations, you may find it all too easy to make unhealthy choices. Your challenge, of course, is to resist those unhealthy temptations by every means you can, including prayer. And rest assured: when you ask for God's help, He will give it.

In the space below, write down the most important choices you can make to improve your health today.

_____

_____

_____

_____

_____

_____

_____

## SHOUT FOR JOY

*Shout triumphantly to the Lord, all the earth. Serve the Lord with gladness; come before Him with joyful songs.*

Psalm 100:1-2 HCSB

The 100th Psalm reminds us that the entire earth should "Shout for joy to the Lord." As you contemplate your faith, your fitness, and your future, don't forget to celebrate the life God has given you. As a Christian, you have been blessed beyond measure. So, make thanksgiving a habit, a regular part of your daily routine. Today, pause and thank your Creator for His blessings. And then demonstrate your gratitude to the Giver of all things good by using His gifts for the glory of His kingdom.

In the space below, write down your thoughts about God's gifts to you and your family.

_____

_____

_____

_____

_____

_____

_____

_____

## KEEP THINGS IN PERSPECTIVE

*Don't copy the behavior and customs of this world, but let God transform you into a new person by changing the way you think. Then you will know what God wants you to do, and you will know how good and pleasing and perfect his will really is.*

Romans 12:2 NLT

If a temporary loss of perspective has robbed you of the spiritual fitness that should be yours in Christ, it's time to readjust your thought patterns. Negative thoughts are habit-forming; thankfully, so are positive ones. With practice, you can form the habit of focusing on God's priorities and your possibilities. When you do, you'll soon discover that you will spend less time fretting about your challenges and more time praising God for His gifts.

In the space below, write down your thoughts on the benefits of putting first things first.

## LOST IN THE CROWD

*The fear of man is a snare, but the one who trusts in the Lord is protected.*

Proverbs 29:25 HCSB

Rick Warren observed, "Those who follow the crowd usually get lost in it." We know these words to be true, but oftentimes we fail to live by them. Instead of trusting God for guidance, we imitate our neighbors and suffer the consequences. Instead of seeking to please our Father in heaven, we strive to please our peers, with decidedly mixed results. Whom will you try to please today: your God or your associates? Your obligation is most certainly not to neighbors, to friends, or even to family members. Your obligation is to an all-knowing, all-powerful God. You must seek to please Him first and always. No exceptions.

In the space below, write down your thoughts about the importance of pleasing God, not people.

_____

_____

_____

_____

_____

_____

## PRAY, BELIEVE, AND ACHIEVE

*Therefore I say to you, whatever things you ask when you pray, believe that you receive them, and you will have them.*

Mark 11:24 NKJV

If you're trying to improve the state of your physical, emotional, or spiritual health, prayer might just be your most powerful tool. In those quiet moments when you open your heart to God, He will give you direction, perspective, wisdom, and courage. He will encourage you to become more fit in a variety of ways: more spiritually fit, more physically fit, and more emotionally fit. God is willing to do His part to ensure that you remain fit. Are you willing to do yours?

In the space below, write down prayer requests concerning your spiritual, emotional, or physical health.

## GOD'S VOICE

*For this is commendable, if because of conscience toward God one endures grief, suffering wrongfully.*

1 Peter 2:19 NKJV

Billy Graham correctly observed, "Most of us follow our conscience as we follow a wheelbarrow. We push it in front of us in the direction we want to go." To do so, of course, is a profound mistake. Yet all of us, on occasion, have failed to listen to the voice that God planted in our hearts, and all of us have suffered the consequences. God gave you a conscience for a very good reason: to make your path conform to His will. So, when your conscience speaks, listen and learn. In all likelihood, God is trying to get His message through. And in all likelihood, it is a message that you desperately need to hear.

In the space below, write down your thoughts about the importance of listening to your conscience.

_____

_____

_____

_____

_____

_____

## JOY AND THE CHRISTIAN LIFE

*Light shines on those who do right; joy belongs to those who are honest. Rejoice in the Lord, you who do right. Praise his holy name.*

Psalm 97:11-12 NCV

God's Word makes it clear: He intends that His joy should become our joy. The Lord intends that believers should share His love with His joy in their hearts. Yet sometimes, amid the inevitable hustle and bustle of life-here-on-earth, we can forfeit—albeit temporarily—God's joy as we wrestle with the challenges of daily living. If, today, your heart is heavy, open the door of your soul to Christ. He will give you peace and joy. And if you already have the joy of Christ in your heart, share it freely, just as Christ freely shared His joy with you.

In the space below, write down your thoughts about Christ's love for you.

_____

_____

_____

_____

_____

_____

## BEYOND MATERIALISM

*For what does it benefit a man to gain the whole world yet lose his life? What can a man give in exchange for his life?*

Mark 8:36-37 HCSB

In our modern society, we need money to live. But as Christians, we must never make the acquisition of money the central focus of our lives. Money is a tool, but it should never overwhelm our sensibilities. The focus of life must be squarely on things spiritual, not things material.

Whenever we place our love for material possessions above our love for God—or when we yield to the countless other temptations of everyday living—we find ourselves engaged in a struggle between good and evil. Let us respond to this struggle by freeing ourselves from that subtle yet powerful temptation: the temptation to love the world more than we love God.

In the space below, write down your thoughts about the dangers of materialism.

_____

_____

_____

_____

_____

## THE LAST WORD

*For God has not given us a spirit of fearfulness, but one of power, love, and sound judgment. So don't be ashamed of the testimony about our Lord, or of me His prisoner. Instead, share in suffering for the gospel, relying on the power of God.*

2 Timothy 1:7-8 HCSB

All of us may find our courage tested by the inevitable disappointments and tragedies of life. After all, ours is a world that seems to be filled with uncertainty, hardship, sickness, and danger.

When we focus upon our fears and our doubts, we may find many reasons to lie awake at night and fret about the uncertainties of the coming day. A better strategy, of course, is to focus not upon our fears, but instead upon our God. God is your shield and your strength. So don't focus your thoughts upon the fears of the day. Instead, trust God's plan and His eternal love for you.

In the space below, write down your thoughts about God's protection.

_____

_____

_____

_____

_____

# THE CHAINS OF PERFECTIONISM

*Those who wait for perfect weather will never plant seeds; those who look at every cloud will never harvest crops.*

Ecclesiastes 11:4 NCV

The media delivers an endless stream of messages that tell you how to look, how to behave, and how to dress. The media's expectations are impossible to meet—God's are not. God doesn't expect perfection . . . and neither should you. If you find yourself bound up by the chains of perfectionism, it's time to ask yourself who you're trying to impress, and why. Your first responsibility is to the Heavenly Father who created you and to His Son who saved you. Then, you bear a powerful responsibility to your family. But, when it comes to meeting society's unrealistic expectations, forget it! After all, pleasing God is simply a matter of obeying His commandments and accepting His Son. But as for pleasing everybody else? That's impossible!

In the space below, write down your thoughts about the dangers of perfectionism.

---

---

---

---

---

## TRUSTING HIM COMPLETELY

*I will be your God throughout your lifetime—until your hair is white with age. I made you, and I will care for you. I will carry you along and save you.*

Isaiah 46:4 NLT

God has promised to lift you up and guide your steps if you let Him do so. God has promised that when you entrust your life to Him completely and without reservation, He will give you the strength to meet any challenge and the wisdom to live in His righteousness.

God's hand uplifts those who turn their hearts and prayers to Him. Will you count yourself among that number? Will you accept God's peace and wear God's armor against the temptations and distractions of our dangerous world? If you do, you can live courageously and optimistically, knowing that you have been forever touched by the loving, unfailing, uplifting hand of God.

In the space below, write down your thoughts about the need to trust God completely.

_____

_____

_____

_____

_____

## RELYING UPON HIM

*Be humble under God's powerful hand so he will lift you up when the right time comes. Give all your worries to him, because he cares about you.*

1 Peter 5:6-7 NCV

God is a never-ending source of support and courage for those of us who call upon Him. When we are weary, He gives us strength. When we see no hope, God reminds us of His promises. When we grieve, God wipes away our tears.

Do the demands of this day threaten to overwhelm you? If so, you must rely not only upon your own resources but also upon the promises of your Father in heaven. God will hold your hand and walk with you every day of your life if you let Him. So even if your circumstances are difficult, trust the Father. His love is eternal and His goodness endures forever.

In the space below, tell God that you will rely on Him today, tomorrow, and forever.

_____

_____

_____

_____

_____

_____

## CHOICES, CHOICES, CHOICES

*Therefore, whether we are at home or away, we make it our aim to be pleasing to Him.*

2 Corinthians 5:9 HCSB

Your life is a series of choices. From the instant you wake up in the morning until the moment you nod off to sleep at night, you make lots of decisions: decisions about the things you do, decisions about the words you speak, decisions about the foods you eat, and decisions about the thoughts you choose to think. Simply put, the quality of those decisions determines the quality of your life. So, if you sincerely want to lead a life that is pleasing to God, you must make choices that are pleasing to Him. He deserves no less . . . and neither, for that matter, do you.

In the space below, write down your thoughts about the rewards of wise choices and the dangers of unwise ones.

_____

_____

_____

_____

_____

_____

_____

## MAKING ACTIONS MATCH BELIEFS

*As you have therefore received Christ Jesus the Lord, so walk in Him, rooted and built up in Him and established in the faith, as you have been taught, abounding in it with thanksgiving.*

Colossians 2:6-7 NKJV

As Christians, we must do our best to make sure that our actions are accurate reflections of our beliefs. Our theology must be demonstrated, not only by our words but, more importantly, by our actions. In short, we should be practical believers, quick to act whenever we see an opportunity to serve God. We may proclaim our beliefs to our hearts' content, but our proclamations will mean nothing—to others or to ourselves—unless we accompany our words with deeds that match.

In the space below, write down your thoughts about the dangers of disobeying God's commandments.

## THE IMPORTANCE OF PRAYER

*Be anxious for nothing, but in everything by prayer and supplication, with thanksgiving, let your requests be made known to God.*

Philippians 4:6 NKJV

Prayer is a powerful tool for improving your health and your life. Prayer is an opportunity to commune with the Giver of all things good. Prayer is not a thing to be taken lightly or to be used infrequently. Prayer should never be reserved for mealtimes or for bedtimes; it should be an ever-present focus in our daily lives. Daily prayer and meditation is a matter of will and habit. You must willingly organize your time by carving out quiet moments with God, and you must form the habit of daily worship. When you do, you'll discover that no time is more precious than the silent moments you spend with your Heavenly Father.

In the space below, write down five things you want to pray about today.

_____

_____

_____

_____

_____

_____

## HIS JOY . . . AND YOURS

*Rejoice in the Lord always. I will say it again: Rejoice!*

Philippians 4:4 HCSB

Corrie ten Boom correctly observed, "Jesus did not promise to change the circumstances around us. He promised great peace and pure joy to those who would learn to believe that God actually controls all things." So here's a prescription for better spiritual health: Learn to trust God, and open the door of your soul to Christ. When you do, He will most certainly give you the peace and pure joy He has promised.

In the space below, write down your thoughts about God's control over His world and yours.

_____

_____

_____

_____

_____

_____

_____

_____

# TURNING AWAY FROM ANGER

*My dear brothers and sisters, always be willing to listen and slow to speak. Do not become angry easily, because anger will not help you live the right kind of life God wants.*

James 1:19-20 NCV

Perhaps God gave each of us one mouth and two ears in order that we might listen twice as much as we speak. Unfortunately, many of us do otherwise, especially when we become angry.

Anger is a natural human emotion that is sometimes necessary and appropriate. Even Jesus Himself became angered when He confronted the moneychangers in the temple. But, more often than not, our frustrations are of the more mundane variety. When you are tempted to lose your temper over the minor inconveniences of life, don't. Turn away from anger, and turn instead to God.

In the space below, write down your thoughts about the dangers of unresolved anger.

_____

_____

_____

_____

_____

## BEING PATIENT WITH YOURSELF

*Knowing God leads to self-control. Self-control leads to patient endurance, and patient endurance leads to godliness.*

2 Peter 1:6 NLT

Being patient with other people can be difficult. But sometimes, we find it even more difficult to be patient with ourselves. We have high expectations and lofty goals. We want to accomplish things now, not later. And, of course, we want our lives to unfold according to our own timetables, not God's. Throughout the Bible, we are instructed that patience is the companion of wisdom. God's message, then, is clear: we must be patient with all people, beginning with that particular person who stares back at us each time we gaze into the mirror.

In the space below, write down your thoughts about the need to be accepting of your own imperfections.

_____

_____

_____

_____

_____

_____

_____

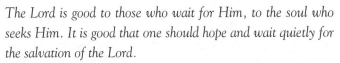

# IN A HURRY?

*The Lord is good to those who wait for Him, to the soul who seeks Him. It is good that one should hope and wait quietly for the salvation of the Lord.*

Lamentations 3:25-26 NKJV

Are you a woman in a hurry? If so, you may be in for a few disappointments. Why? Because life has a way of unfolding according to God's timetable, not yours. That's why life requires patience . . . and lots of it!

For most of us, waiting quietly for God is difficult because we're in such a hurry for things to happen! The next time you find your patience tested to the limit, slow down and trust God. Sometimes, we must wait patiently for Him, and that's as it should be. After all, think about how patient God has been with us.

In the space below, write down your thoughts about the rewards of patience.

## BE STILL

*Be still, and know that I am God.*

Psalm 46:10 NKJV

We live in a noisy world, a world filled with distractions, frustrations, obligations, and complications. But we must not allow our clamorous world to separate us from God's peace. Instead, we must "be still" so that we might sense the presence of God. If we are to maintain clear minds and compassionate hearts, we must take time each day for prayer and for meditation. We must make ourselves still in the presence of our Creator. We must quiet our minds and our hearts so that we might sense God's will, God's path, and God's love.

In the space below, write down your thoughts about the value of spending quiet moments each day with God.

_____

_____

_____

_____

_____

_____

_____

## LIFETIME LEARNING

*The wise person makes learning a joy; fools spout only foolishness.*

Proverbs 15:2 NLT

When it comes to learning life's lessons, we can either do things the easy way or the hard way. The easy way can be summed up as follows: when God teaches us a lesson, we learn it . . . the first time! Unfortunately, many of us learn much more slowly than that. When we resist God's instruction, He continues to teach, whether we like it or not. And, if we keep making the same old mistakes, God responds by rewarding us with the same old results. Hopefully, we learn those lessons sooner rather than later because the sooner we do, the sooner He can move on to the next lesson and the next, and the next . . .

God still has important lessons to teach you. In the space below, write down at least one lesson that God may be trying to teach you.

_____

_____

_____

_____

_____

## MAKING THE CHOICE
## TO CARE FOR YOUR BODY

*Do you not know that your body is a sanctuary of the Holy Spirit who is in you, whom you have from God? You are not your own, for you were bought at a price; therefore glorify God in your body.*

1 Corinthians 6:19-20 HCSB

God asks that we slow down long enough to think about the choices that we make, and He asks that we make those choices in accordance with His commandments. The Bible teaches us that our bodies are "temples" which belong to God (1 Corinthians 6:19-20). We are commanded (not encouraged, not advised, commanded!) to treat our bodies with respect and honor. We do so by making wise choices and by making those choices consistently over an extended period of time.

In the space below, assure God that you will continue to care for the body He has given you.

_____

_____

_____

_____

_____

## TRUST GOD, BE HAPPY

*The one who trusts in the Lord will be happy.*

Proverbs 16:20 HCSB

The Scottish preacher George McDonald observed, "It has been well said that no man ever sank under the burden of the day. It is when tomorrow's burden is added to the burden of today that the weight is more than a man can bear. Never load yourselves so, my friends. If you find yourselves so loaded, at least remember this: it is your own doing, not God's. He begs you to leave the future to Him." Today, as a gift to yourself, to your family, and to your friends, claim the inner peace that is your spiritual birthright: the peace of Jesus Christ. Christ is standing at the door, waiting patiently for you to invite Him to reign over your heart. His eternal peace is offered freely. Claim it today.

In the space below, write down a few things you're worried about, and then turn those worries over to God. You can trust Him to protect you.

_____

_____

_____

_____

_____

## THE RIGHT KIND OF EXAMPLE

*You should be an example to the believers in speech, in conduct, in love, in faith, in purity.*

1 Timothy 4:12 HCSB

Whether you know it or not, you're a role model. Your friends and family members watch your actions and make careful mental notes. Your obligation, of course, is to behave accordingly. After all, your words of instruction will never ring true unless you yourself are willing to follow them. Phillips Brooks advised, "Be such a man, and live such a life, that if every person were such as you, and every life a life like yours, this earth would be God's Paradise." That's sound advice for men and women alike because your family and friends are watching.

If you make healthy habits an important part of your own lifestyle, your close family members will, in all likelihood, follow your example. In the space below, write your thoughts about the importance of being a good role model for your family.

---

---

---

---

---

## THE SEEDS OF GENEROSITY

*Freely you have received, freely give.*

Matthew 10:8 NKJV

Paul reminds us that when we sow the seeds of generosity, we reap bountiful rewards in accordance with God's plan for our lives. Thus, we are instructed to give cheerfully and without reservation: "But this I say, He which soweth sparingly shall reap also sparingly; and he which soweth bountifully shall reap also bountifully. Every man according as he purposeth in his heart, so let him give; not grudgingly, or of necessity: for God loveth a cheerful giver" (2 Corinthians 9:6, 7 KJV). Today, make this pledge and keep it: Be a cheerful, generous, courageous giver. The world needs your help, and you need the spiritual rewards that will be yours when you give it.

In the space below, write down the name of at least one person who needs your help today. And jot down ways you can help . . . today.

_____

_____

_____

_____

_____

_____

## GREAT IS HIS FAITHFULNESS

*God is faithful, by whom you were called into the fellowship of His Son, Jesus Christ our Lord.*

1 Corinthians 1:9 NKJV

God is faithful to us even when we are not faithful to Him. God keeps His promises to us even when we stray far from His will. He continues to love us even when we disobey His commandments. But God does not force His blessings upon us. If we are to experience His love and His grace, we must claim them for ourselves. Are you tired, discouraged, or fearful? Be comforted: God is with you. Are you confused? Listen to the quiet voice of your Heavenly Father. Are you bitter? Talk with God and seek His guidance. Are you celebrating a great victory? Thank God and praise Him. He is the Giver of all things good. In whatever condition you find yourself, trust God and be comforted. The Father is with you now and forever.

In the space below, write down your thoughts about God's faithfulness.

_____

_____

_____

_____

_____

# NEW BEGINNINGS

*Then the One seated on the throne said, "Look! I am making everything new."*

Revelation 21:5 HCSB

Each new day offers countless opportunities to serve God, to seek His will, and to obey His teachings. But each day also offers countless opportunities to stray from God's commandments and to wander far from His path. Sometimes, we wander aimlessly in a wilderness of our own making, but God has better plans for us. And, whenever we ask Him to renew our strength and guide our steps, He does so. Consider this day a new beginning. Consider it a fresh start, a renewed opportunity to serve your Creator with willing hands and a loving heart. Ask God to renew your sense of purpose as He guides your steps. Today is a glorious opportunity to serve God. Seize that opportunity while you can; tomorrow may indeed be too late.

In the space below, write down what you think God's purpose for you is and how you might better serve Him.

_____

_____

_____

_____

_____

## ACCEPTING LIFE

*Do not remember the past events, pay no attention to things of old. Look, I am about to do something new; even now it is coming. Do you not see it? Indeed, I will make a way in the wilderness, rivers in the desert.*

Isaiah 43:18-19 HCSB

As human beings with limited comprehension, we can never fully understand the will of our Father in Heaven. But as believers in a benevolent God, we must always trust His providence. When Jesus went to the Mount of Olives, as described in Luke 22, He poured out His heart to God. Jesus knew of the agony that He was destined to endure, but He also knew that God's will must be done. Like Christ, we too must ultimately seek God's will, not our own.

Today, write down at least one aspect of your life that you've been reluctant to accept, and then prayerfully ask God to help you trust Him more by accepting the past.

_____

_____

_____

_____

_____

_____

## THANKSGIVING YES . . . ENVY NO!

*Stop your anger! Turn from your rage! Do not envy others—it only leads to harm.*

Psalm 37:8 NLT

As the recipient of God's grace, you have every reason to celebrate life. After all, God has promised you the opportunity to receive His abundance and His joy—in fact, you have the opportunity to receive those gifts right now. But if you allow envy to gnaw away at the fabric of your soul, you'll find that joy remains elusive. So do yourself an enormous favor: Rather than succumbing to the sin of envy, focus on the marvelous things that God has done for you—starting with Christ's sacrifice. Thank the Giver of all good gifts, and keep thanking Him for the wonders of His love and the miracles of His creation. Count your own blessings and let your neighbors count theirs. It's the godly way to live.

In the space below, write down your thoughts about the dangers of envy.

_____

_____

_____

_____

_____

## EXCELLENCE, NOT EXCUSES

*And now, children, stay with Christ. Live deeply in Christ. Then we'll be ready for him when he appears, ready to receive him with open arms, with no cause for red-faced guilt or lame excuses when he arrives.*

1 John 2:28-29 MSG

We live in a world where excuses are everywhere. And it's precisely because excuses are so numerous that they are also so ineffective. When we hear the words, "I'm sorry but . . . ," most of us know exactly what is to follow: the excuse. Because we humans are such creative excuse-makers, all of the really good excuses have already been taken. That's why excuses don't work—we've heard them all before. So, if you're wasting your time trying to concoct a new and improved excuse, don't bother. It's impossible. A far better strategy is this: do the work. Now. And let your excellent work speak loudly and convincingly for itself.

In the space below, write down your thoughts about the futility of making excuses.

## SENSING HIS PRESENCE

*Where can I go from your Spirit? Where can I flee from your presence? If I go up to the heavens, you are there; if I make my bed in the depths, you are there. If I rise on the wings of the dawn, if I settle on the far side of the sea, even there your hand will guide me, your right hand will hold me fast.*

Psalm 139:7-10 NIV

If God is everywhere, why does He sometimes seem so far away? The answer to that question, of course, has nothing to do with God and everything to do with us. When we begin each day on our knees, in praise and worship to Him, God often seems very near indeed. But, if we ignore God's presence or—worse yet—rebel against it altogether, the world in which we live becomes a spiritual wasteland. Wherever you are, whether you are happy or sad, victorious or vanquished, celebrate God's presence. And be comforted. For He is here.

In the space below, jot down a few thoughts about God's love for you and your family.

_____

_____

_____

_____

_____

# YOUR SPIRITUAL JOURNEY

*I pray that you, being rooted and firmly established in love, may be able to comprehend with all the saints what is the breadth and width, height and depth, and to know the Messiah's love that surpasses knowledge, so you may be filled with all the fullness of God.*

Ephesians 3:17-19 HCSB

The journey toward spiritual maturity lasts a lifetime. As Christians, we can and should continue to grow in the love and the knowledge of our Savior as long as we live. When we cease to grow, either emotionally or spiritually, we do ourselves a profound disservice. Each day, we make countless decisions that can bring us closer to God. When we live according to the principles contained in God's Holy Word, we embark upon a journey of spiritual maturity that results in life abundant and life eternal.

In the space below, write down at least one thing you can do today to aid in your spiritual growth.

_____

_____

_____

_____

_____

## TODAY'S OPPORTUNITIES

*But encourage each other daily, while it is still called today, so that none of you is hardened by sin's deception.*

Hebrews 3:13 HCSB

The 118th Psalm reminds us, "This is the day which the Lord hath made; we will rejoice and be glad in it" (v. 24 KJV). As we rejoice in this day that the Lord has given us, let us remember that an important part of today's celebration is the time we spend celebrating others. Each day provides countless opportunities to encourage others and to praise their good works. When we do, we not only spread seeds of happiness, we also follow the commandments of God's Holy Word. So look for the good in others and celebrate the good that you find. When you do, you'll be a powerful force of encouragement in the world and a worthy servant to your God.

In the space below, write down the names of a few people who need your encouragement today.

_____

_____

_____

_____

_____

## LIFE'S ROADMAP

*All Scripture is inspired by God and is profitable for teaching, for rebuking, for correcting, for training in righteousness, so that the man of God may be complete, equipped for every good work.*

2 Timothy 3:16-17 HCSB

God's Word is unlike any other book. The Bible is a road-map for life here on earth and for life eternal. As Christians, we are called upon to study God's Holy Word, to trust its promises, to follow its commandments, and to share its Good News with the world. God's Holy Word is, indeed, a life-changing, one-of-a-kind treasure. And, a passing acquaintance with the Good Book is insufficient for Christians who seek to obey God's Word and to understand His will.

In the space below, write down a few thoughts about the role that the Bible plays in your life.

_____

_____

_____

_____

_____

_____

# FAITH THAT MOVES MOUNTAINS

*I assure you: If anyone says to this mountain, "Be lifted up and thrown into the sea," and does not doubt in his heart, but believes that what he says will happen, it will be done for him.*

Mark 11:23 HCSB

Because we live in a demanding world, all of us have mountains to climb and mountains to move. Moving those mountains requires faith. Are you a mountain mover whose faith is evident for all to see? Hopefully so. God needs more women who are willing to move mountains for His glory and for His kingdom. God walks with you, ready and willing to strengthen you. Accept His strength today. And remember—Jesus taught His disciples that if they had faith, they could move mountains. You can too . . . so with no further ado, let the mountain-moving begin.

In the space below, write down your thoughts about the power of faith.

_____

_____

_____

_____

_____

_____

## THE LOVE OF MONEY

*For the love of money is a root of all kinds of evil, and by craving it, some have wandered away from the faith and pierced themselves with many pains.*

1 Timothy 6:10 HCSB

Our society is in love with money and the things that money can buy. God is not. God cares about people, not possessions, and so must we. Money, in and of itself, is not evil; worshipping money is. So today, as you prioritize matters of importance for you and yours, remember that God is almighty, but the dollar is not. If we worship God, we are blessed. But if we worship "the almighty dollar," we are inevitably punished because of our misplaced priorities—and our punishment usually comes sooner rather than later.

In the space below, write down your thoughts about at least one way to show others that God rules your heart not money.

_____

_____

_____

_____

_____

## OBSERVING THE SABBATH

*But an hour is coming, and is now here, when the true worshipers will worship the Father in spirit and truth. Yes, the Father wants such people to worship Him. God is Spirit, and those who worship Him must worship in spirit and truth.*

John 4:23-24 HCSB

When God gave Moses the Ten Commandments, it became perfectly clear that our Heavenly Father intends for us to make the Sabbath a holy day, a day for worship, for contemplation, for fellowship, and for rest. Yet we live in a seven-day-a-week world, a world that all too often treats Sunday as a regular workday. One way to strengthen your faith is by giving God at least one day each week. If you carve out the time for a day of worship and praise, you'll be amazed at the impact it will have on the rest of your week.

In the space below, write down several new ways you and your family can honor God on the Sabbath.

## GIVE HIM YOUR HEART

*For God so loved the world that He gave His only begotten Son, that whoever believes in Him should not perish but have everlasting life.*

God's love for you is deeper and more profound than you can imagine. God's love for you is so great that He sent His only Son to this earth to die for your sins and to offer you the priceless gift of eternal life. Now, you must decide whether or not to accept God's gift. Will you ignore it or embrace it? Will you accept Christ's love and build a life-long relationship with Him, or will you turn away from Him and take a different path?

Accept God's gift now: allow His Son to preside over your heart, your thoughts, and your life, starting this very instant.

The ultimate choice for you is the choice to invite God's Son into your heart. In the space below, thank Christ for His sacrifice on the cross and for the gift of eternal life.

_____

_____

_____

_____

# COMMISSIONED TO WITNESS

*Go, therefore, and make disciples of all nations, baptizing them in the name of the Father and of the Son and of the Holy Spirit, teaching them to observe everything I have commanded you. And remember, I am with you always, to the end of the age.*

Matthew 28:19-20 HCSB

---

After His resurrection, Jesus addressed His disciples. As recorded in the 28th chapter of Matthew, Christ instructed His followers to share His message with the world. This "Great Commission" applies to Christians of every generation, including our own. As believers, we are called to share the Good News of Jesus with our families, with our neighbors, and with the world. Christ commanded His disciples to become fishers of men. We must do likewise, and we must do so today. Tomorrow may indeed be too late.

---

The best day to respond to Christ's Great Commission is this day. In the space below, write down the name of at least one person with whom you will share your testimony today.

_____

_____

_____

_____

_____

# NOTES

# NOTES

# NOTES

# NOTES